ALASKA
NORTHWEST
ARCTIC HUNTS

Multi-Species Hunts in the Northwest Arctic

JAKE JACOBSON

Alaska's Favorite Real Life Wilderness Storyteller

PUBLICATION CONSULTANTS
We Believe In The Power Of Authors

PO Box 221974 Anchorage, Alaska 99522-1974
books@publicationconsultants.com—www.publicationconsultants.com

ISBN 978-1-63747-091-6

eBook ISBN Number: 978-1-63747-092-3

Library of Congress Number: 2022905331

Copyright 2022 Jake Jacobson

—First Edition—

All rights reserved, including the right of reproduction in any form, or by any mechanical or electronic means including photocopying or recording, or by any information storage or retrieval system, in whole or in part in any form, and in any case not without the written permission of the author.
J.P. "Jake" Jacobson
Alaska Master Guide #54
PO Box 1313
Kodiak, Alaska 99615
website: www.huntfish.us/
email: huntfish@ak.net

Manufactured in the United States of America

ALASKA Northwest Arctic Hunts
is the seventh book by Jake Jacobson on Alaskan topics.
His other books are:

ALASKA HUNTING: Earthworms to Elephants

ALASKA TALES: Laughs and Surprises

ALASKA FLYING: Surviving Incidents and Accidents

ALASKA BEARS: Stirred and Shaken

KODIAK ALASKA DEER: Stories, Sterility and Stewardship

ALASKA CARIBOU: Ramblings & Ruminations

Jake's books can be found at amazon.com and other good book stores or autographed copies can be ordered directly from Jake.

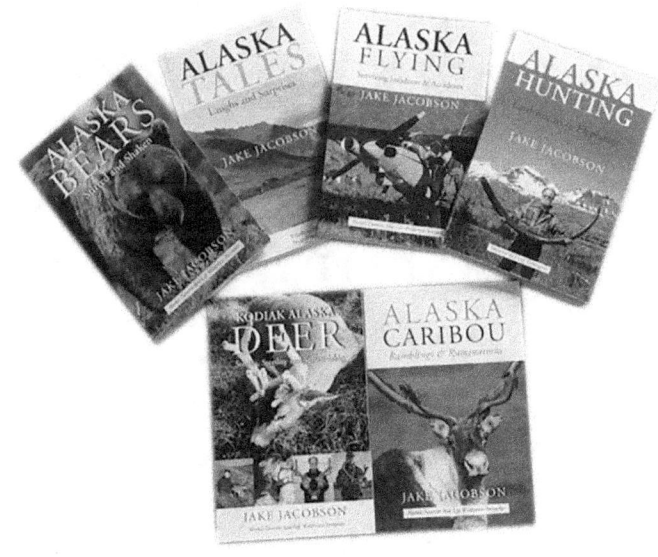

Contents

Foreword 7

Introduction
Multiple Species Hunts 9

1979–1980
Mixed Bag Hunt 19

1980–1982
Ulrich and Heiner 51

The Narcoleptic Visitor 73

Some Events of 1984 101

An African Professional Hunter Guest 109

Grizzlies, Raven, And The Snow Snake 117

Two Brothers From West Germany 127

Mac, Will, Max and Me 143

1989
Multiple Species Hunts
after a TOUGH WINTER 167

A Double on Grizzlies 193

2012
The Fall Season 213

Foreword

A couple of months ago, I got an email from my friend and outfitter, Jake Jacobson. Jake let me know that he was putting the finishing touches on the seventh book of his Alaska series. He asked me to write a foreword to it. I was extremely flattered, and immediately shot back an email accepting the project.

Most writers of book forewords are famous in their own right, usually because they are noted writers, or are renowned in the field that is the subject of the book. I'm not. I am not famous, not even close. I'm not a great writer. I'm not a writer at all. While I dabble in big game hunting, I'm not a famous hunter. The only qualification I can think of is, I really like Jake's stories. Jake knows that. I have copies of all his previous books. I've read and re-read them until they are dog-eared.

Thinking about that led me to think about what it is that I like about Jake's stories. I'd really never stopped to think about it before. I mean, I like them; I'm not a particularly deep thinker, and that had always been enough. This time, though, I thought it might be good to examine the "why."

If you're picking up this book thinking you're going to catch the next Nobel laureate in literature, you're probably out of luck. Jake isn't Hemingway. Now, in my book, that's a good thing, because I think Hemingway was a lousy writer. Jake's stories don't have layers and layers of meaning, to be peeled away one by one, only to discover that there is nothing at the core. These are straightforward fireside yarns. The ones that are supposed to be funny are funny. The scary ones are scary. The heartwarming ones, well, you get the picture. Jake has an engaging, conversational style. The substance of his stories is drawn from the seemingly inexhaustible trove of his adventurous, unconventional life. I love Jake's stories because they speak to me in a very direct way about things that are important to me.

I think Jake recognizes that I feel that way about his stories. So, he asked me to write a forward not because I'm famous, but because I'm one of you, the people for whom these stories were written. I hope you'll trust me on this. I think, like me, you'll really enjoy this book. These stories are for us, and Jake Jacobson is our voice. Thanks, Jake.

Introduction
Multiple Species Hunts

Often, when looking at the vast wild country I get the feeling that it is immutable and unchanging, enduring forever. But in my lifetime I have seen many significant changes.

Since I first saw northwest Arctic Alaska in 1967, I've witnessed some dramatic changes in game populations, cost of licenses and tags, seasons and bag limits, and of course the weather and climate.

When I first came to Trail Creek - approximately 157 miles north of the Arctic Circle - in 1967 - large Aufis glaciers formed every year upstream and downstream from the location I picked for the homestead site. Most years the ice remained throughout the summer only to build anew and thicker in September.

The lodge sits to the left (East) of the middle one. These ice sheets make surface travel hazardous for humans and therefore, provide good security for the lodge buildings. I have never felt the need of a "winter or

Late July: Looking south are three large Aufis glaciers.

security man." The aufis glaciers remained super cold throughout the summer, but by 1990 we no longer had winter Aufis to use much after the end of August.

Travel on Aufis is risky, at best. Often undercut areas are impossible to discern. A person on a snow machine - or on foot - may suddenly break through.

Teresa is amused by so much ice in late August, 1988.

Dog teams are reluctant to travel on aufis.

Multiple Species Hunts

This lake eroded the permafrost and drained itself.

Lakes are scattered throughout the country and frequently the subsurface drainage eats itself through the underlying permafrost and spontaneously drains the lake. Many lakes upon which I formerly landed my float plane, are now just flat mud pans. Some of the larger ones dried out so thoroughly that I have been able to land a wheel plane on what formerly was a lake.

Erosion along rivers and ocean beaches often exposes a frost melt-out such as shown below. This one, about fifteen miles downstream from the lodge, coughed up a large Wooly Mammoth tusk and some bones.

Frost melt-out on a river bank.

Apparently the flat appearing tundra began formation as an ancient river delta deposit which accumulated carcasses of mammoths and other animals of the last ice age. Permafrost formed in the moist organic components of the soil which then preserved the carcasses for millenia, until finally they were exposed to ambient air temperatures. Some "melt-outs" like this emit odors reminiscent of a horse barn at noon.

Earth has experienced cold periods (or "ice ages") and warm periods ("interglacials") on roughly 100,000-year cycles for at least the last one million years. The last of these ice ages ended around 10,000 to 20,000 years ago which resulted in the most recent great megafauna extinction, eliminating Pleistocene species such as wooly mammoths, ancient bison, saber toothed cats, sloth bears, and scores of other large, charismatic megafauna, along with countless smaller creatures.

Palentologists tell us with confidence that, in all there were five mass extinction events, beginning with the **Ordovician-Silurian extinction** (corals and shelled brachiopods) about 440 million years ago - we find fossilized coral heads in northwest Arctic Alaska from this event.

Coral heads vary from baseball to a small car in size.

The **Late Devonian extinction** (the age fo fish) around 365 million years ago,

The **Permian-Triassic extinction** (first appearance of land mammals) which took place 253 million years ago and eliminated 96% of marine life and 70% of terrestrial species and the **Triassic-Jurassic extinction** of 201 million years ago wiped out some 90% of all the planet's species. This is called "the great dying."

Finally the **K-Pg or Cretaceous-Paleogene extinction** of 66 million years ago erased 75% of the species on earth, including the great dinosaurs. The many wooly mammoth remains we find are due to the later part of this die-off.

Some say we are witnessing the sixth mass extinction now which began approximately 10,000 years ago.

School of ancient fish preserved in stone.

Some of the mammoth tusks I found were suitable only for jewelry.

So we are living in and experiencing a warming period on an ever changing planet. We are "Interglacial Men."

Moose were not part of the natural fauna in the Kotzebue area prior to 1955 when five moose from the Koyukuk River country entered the Selawik/Kobuk headwaters. This information was given to me by a federal government hunter who primarily shot wolves that threatened local reindeer.

Moose was a new animal to most local people. It was so unfamiliar to local Inuits that they had no unique name for the animal. The Inuit language word for Moose is Tutupuk, which literally means big Caribou.

The fellow who was employed by the Federal government to protect the local native-owned reindeer from wolves took it upon himself to shoot every predator that potentially threatened those moose. He told me that he even shot eagles when he found the big raptors near young calves.

It's been my observation that wolves and bears must learn to effectively prey on moose, which may take some time. For wolves it requires a much different strategy to bring down a moose weighing three quarters of a ton, than that used for a caribou which may weigh up to three hundred and fifty pounds.

In good browsing conditions cow moose normally produce two calves per year, so the learning curve of the large predators, coupled with the high reproduction rate of moose and excellent browse, was favorable for the big, slow, ungulates to proliferate. Moose rapidly spread throughout the northwestern parts of Alaska.

The moose found the theretofore exuberant, unbrowsed willows and the as yet un-practiced wolves and bears to be conducive to rapid expansion of their population. After twenty years in northwest Alaska, moose had expanded throughout Game Management Unit 23, and westward to populate the Seward Peninsula. Population numbers were large and antler development was greater than average. These facts were attributable to the excellent willow growths throughout the area, the unpracticed predators and the abundant *Alces gigas* population.

So, good nutrition, genetics and age led to large antlers. By the late 1970s, northwest Alaska provided perhaps the best trophy moose hunting in the world.

Transportation of hunters soon mushroomed, bringing hundreds of hunters to the area. At times, especially in September, visitors outnumbered the local hunters. Most transported hunters were after the largest antlered animals they could find, but most would take a yearling bull with miniature - even first year - antlers rather than go home with nothing. I was one of many to urge the Alaska Department of Fish and Game to place reasonable limits on the number of people a Transporter could drop off in any year and minimal size limits on bull moose antlers. Eventually a fifty inch spread and/or four projection points on the brow tines of at least one antler were set as bull moose antler minimums. But the regulation came at least fifteen years too late, in my opinion. From an open season of August 1 to March 31, moose are now restricted to local subsistence qualified hunters only and the season runs from July 1 to December 31. The number of Transported hunters is not limited.

Polar bears were plentiful and aggressively hunted from late February through April until passage of the Marine Mammals Protection Act of October, 1972. After that, Polar bears were legally hunted and harvested only by coastal dwelling Alaska Natives.

Grizzly bears and wolves were plentiful and often taken as a bonus for polar bear hunters who had the desire and money. After closure of polar bear hunting to non-natives, two notorious guides continued to come to the Arctic to hunt grizzly bears and wolves. The Alaska Department of Fish and Game was concerned about these fellows same day airborne spring harvests but never could effectively control or monitor their activities, so in 1980 a lottery drawn permit was required for any non resident to hunt grizzly bears in GMU23. The drawing requirement effectively shut down the illegal spring harvest, but the grizzly population expanded so much that the survival of the moose population was put in jeopardy. After thirty-nine years the grizzly drawing was cancelled in 2019 and tags could once again be purchased over the counter.

Grizzly hunters had been limited to one bear every four years, which was liberalized to one bear every year, and two bears per year for residents of GMU23. Additionally from an open season date of September 1, the season was opened on August 1 each year.

Caribou inhabiting GMU23 were part of the the Western Arctic Caribou Herd - WACH. With an estimated population of 242,000 in 1972, there was no closed season and no limit on caribou - and the meat could be sold openly on the market.

In 1976 the WACH underwent a precipitous drop in population to an estimated 75,000 animals - or less. This was primarily due to gross wanton waste by residents of GMU23. However with bag limits - large as they were - and a sudden increase in scrutiny of hunting practices, the WACH grew in population by about thirteen percent per year. By the first decade of the second millennium the WACH population was estimated at 490,000.

An estimated 12,000 WACH caribou are harvested by local subsistence hunters annually, with 250 to 300 taken by non-local hunters.

Dall sheep were never as numerous in the western Brooks Range as I observed while doing government charter flights in the eastern Brooks Range, but there were harvestable populations. People in areas east of GMU23 did customarily harvest Dall sheep for subsistence, but sheep were taken opportunistically by locals in GMU23, and only occasionally.

From the 1960s through 1994, approximately 20 Dall rams were reported as harvested annually in GMU23. In 1994 Federal Subsistence Regulations allowed qualified local subsistence hunters to take Dall sheep from August 1 through April 30. The actual numbers of subsistence harvested Dall sheep are not available, because data was not actively sought by the department of fish and game, however sheep populations plummeted in areas accessible by snow machine with season open nine months. Sport hunting of Dall rams was closed from 1994 until 2004 when eleven sport hunting permits were issued. On numerous occasions during the closure I counted up to one hundred Dall sheep from the windows of the lodge. My permitted guest hunters were 100% successful on harvesting a permitted Dall ram until all hunting - even subsistence hunting - of Dall sheep in GMU23 was closed in 2014. A series of difficult winters with thawing followed by ice formation had led to a huge winter kill in the western Brooks Range. The Dall sheep populations are slowly recovering.

Black bears are plentiful in some parts of GMU23 with a limit of three bears per person per year. But a huge increase in grizzly numbers became evident in the mid 1980s, I have not seen a black bear around the lodge since 1978. I believe grizzlies kill and eat black bears.

Wolf populations have remained essentially stable with a high population, and an annual limit of twenty wolves on a hunting license.

Wolverine with a limit of 1 per year seem stable with a low population level.

Land otters, *Lutra canadensis*, population seem stable at low numbers.

Muskoxen, introduced to the Seward Peninsula and the northwest Arctic coast near Point Hope have prospered and we see small herds occasionally throughout the region. I commonly see old, lone bulls near the lodge, but only local subsistence qualified people are allowed to hunt them.

In one of my previous books, *KODIAK ALASKA DEER: Stories, Sterility and Stewardship*, I detailed the increase in cryptorchidism in Sitka Blacktail Deer in the Kodiak Archipelago - up to 70% in some areas. Andrologists tell me this is probably due to an endocrine mimic or interruptor, which is likely due to industrial contaminants.

Beaver (Castor canadensis) were common on the Kobuk River and further south, but they began to appear on the Noatak River in the late 1970s. In 1979 I noticed a large beaver house on Popple Creek, about five miles down stream from the lodge, but I have not seen other signs of beaver on Trail Creek.

Willow ptarmigan (*Lagopus lagopus*) are common throughout GMU23, however in the last twenty years I have seen progressively fewer birds. Huge flocks used to come from the North Slope (just eight miles north of the lodge) flying in tight formations numbering in the thousands of birds. I have not seen such huge flocks for more than twenty years.

Raptor numbers seem to be stable with Golden Eagles, Merlins, Marsh Hawks, Short eared owls, and Northern Shrike making appearances as normal.

In 2002 and again in 2014 we observed a single American Three-Toed Woodpecker at the lodge and in both years the bird put several holes in the plywood siding of the lodge.

We commonly see Snow Buntings, Northern Wheat Ears and Robins near the lodge.

Snowshoe hares cycle dramatically. The hare population peaked in 1980. Near Kotzebue, I could collect 200 hares in an afternoon with a .22 rifle - most of which I fed to our 32 husky dogs. That spring I noticed bloody diarrhea deposits. I did not see a hare on Trail Creek again until 2004. The hare population remains low on Trail Creek.

Arctic Hares are spotty throughout mainland Alaska. I sighted one on Trail Creek in the 1980. Seward Peninsula has a more dependable population of Arctic Hares. I occasionally found them on Bear Creek near Granite Mountain and I found hundreds of hares on the Goodhope River in March - several years in a row.

Lynx tracks are seen occasionally on Trail Creek, especially after a year or two of high hare populations, and I have seen a single lynx on only two occasions in more than fifty years.

Red foxes are present annually, but never in large numbers. Arctic foxes are seen on rare occasions.

Arctic Char and Grayling are always present in Trail Creek, as well as are small sculpin. Trail Creek is a major spawning stream for the char which come in during July through August, spawn and then attempt to get back down stream before freeze up. Grayling are year-round residents.

Previously I mentioned the aufis glaciers near the lodge have not been forming and lasting throughout the season since about 1990. The autumn freeze-up seems to be coming later.

This warming trend may be responsible for the caribou coming south later each year. A few years ago, the first week in September saw hundreds of GMU23 human residents converge on the Kobuk River upstream from the village of Kiana to intercept and harvest migrating caribou. But caribou are crossing the Kobuk later and in some years there is apparently little movement south of the Kobuk.

Caribou management biologists use radio collars and prefer to have about one hundred animals of the Western Arctic Caribou Herd carry collars. In past decades, biologists captured and collared caribou as they swam across the Kobuk River. In the spring on 2021, with far fewer than a hundred collared caribou, and deep, soft snow conditions, helicopters and net guns were used to place fifty-four new collars. «This collaring method will likely be used again in coming years unless river capture becomes feasible again," the biologists say.

In the past few years I have seen white sox on Trail Creek, whereas in my first forty years in the Arctic I never saw that irksome insect north of the Kobuk River. Mosquitos are stable in large numbers.

So change is taking place on Trail Creek and similar areas of northwest Arctic Alaska in the western Brooks Range.

I wish I could convey to the reader the wonderful smells emitted by Hudson Bay Tea as it is walked upon, the special light quality of an Arctic sunset and the profound sense of silence and being right with the world that I and others feel when at Trail Creek, but my ability as a word wrangler is too limited to adequately do those things.

1979–1980
Mixed Bag Hunt

In 1979 I spent more time flying for the Alaska Department of Fish and Game than I did guiding guest hunters. Bookings were slow that year for most guides I talked with on the subject, so I was pleased to have the work with ADF&G. Whether guiding or working with biologists, it was all interesting to me and it all helped pay the bills.

A fellow from Ohio contracted with me for a mixed bag hunt. He wanted to take a Moose, a Grizzly and a Caribou, prioritized in that order. None of the big game available in my areas required a permit issued by drawing in those days. All non resident and alien big game tags were available over the counter, and I had a vendorship for licenses and tags. That made booking easier and simplified the hunts.

But, in addition to the hunting license, a metal locking tag had to be purchased before any animal could be legally hunted. The round trip from the lodge to Kotzebue was a minimum of three hours in the super cub. Also it was illegal to hunt big game, except caribou, or guide for any big game on the same day airborne. It made sense that I have a Vendor's license so I could sell tags and licenses at the lodge, rather than make the three hour trip to town each time a hunter wanted to take another animal. The simple paper work was not much of a burden and it saved us the considerable expense of going to town and allowed us to hunt every day. Many of the optional animals that were taken would not have been collected if we did not have that Vendor's license. It served us well and was a huge service for out guests.

Mae and I had been at Trail Creek for ten days. We had only the small cabin at first which had been twelve feet square, but I had added an eight foot two-story addition that summer. The back eight feet had a second story bedroom which allowed us and up to three guests to sleep inside with comfortable privacy, and safe from bears.

The day before the hunt was to begin, I flew to Kotzebue to pick up the hunter, named Dave. The Wien Airlines jet arrived in Kotzebue too late for me to get back to the lodge, so I put him up for the night in our spare bedroom. He was tired from his long journey from Ohio and went to sleep early.

The fight

A book I was reading helped me wind down before going to bed, when the phone rang. A friend called me from the hotel bar and offered to buy me a beer. This fellow was an aircraft mechanic that had helped with the installation of a replacement engine when I had a failure on the north slope three years before. I jumped in the Bronco and went to see him.

As we were visiting a disturbance erupted from one of the booths. As the yelling grew louder someone said they thought the guy was hollering at me.

Leaving my unfinished beer, I walked over to the booth. The belligerent fellow screamed that he was going to kill me, as he clutched a beer bottle.

Any alcoholic drink makes me more mellow than usual and I had just swallowed two beers, so I took this guy and his threat with a grain of salt. I told the stranger that I didn't know who he was, but I would buy us each a beer and he could explain who he thought I was, - I laughed - and why he wanted to do me in.

I figured he had me mixed up with someone else.

As I turned my head to order the brews, the guy threw his bottle and it hit me in the cheek. That made me angry!

"Okay, if you think you want to try to take me, let's go outside," I told him.

It was raining when I went out the door and down the steps.

My antagonist came out in a rush, but slipped on the top step and his butt landed on the ground. I stood off, waiting for him to get up.

Two of the men that were in the booth with him grabbed his arms and got him on his feet. He lurched at me with a wild haymaker swing, but I stepped back and his swing missed me. Then, to my surprise, someone grabbed me from behind and held tight, pinning my arms to my sides in a bear hug. The crazy fellow landed two or three knuckle blows on my face. I saw stars with each blow.

Some of my buddies came over to force the guys holding me to let go. I was only vaguely aware of that action.

When the guy holding me let go I was still getting hit repeatedly - mostly in the head - by my wild antagonist, who seemed to be sobering up. I had to get in close to stop the pounding. I moved in and grabbed his shirt, then I began to deliver some jabs to his mid section.

It was a crazy, ugly thing - the two of us struggling out there in the rain and mud. The bar emptied as all the patrons went outside in the rain, taking in the brawl. It was the best entertainment available.

Our wild pugilistic waltz took us across the street and when we were close to an old World War Two weapons carrier, we both fell to the ground. My assailant had quit punching, but I kept jabbing him anywhere I could land my fists. I had a lot of catching up to do.

We rolled under the old Dodge with the lunatic holding tight to me, as I pounded the sides of his head. I got a grip on his ears with both hands and jammed his head up into the under carriage of the vehicle. He let out a holler and I brought his head back to my belly for more upward thrusts. After several such thrusts, when I brought his bloodied head down to my mid section, he bit me and kept his jaws clamped shut on my belly skin.

Now, that really hurt and made me more angry. I wanted to be out from under that Dodge and I wanted the exquisite biting pain on my belly to end. I tried to gouge my thumb into his eyes, but he kept them tightly closed. So I jammed my index finger up his nose as far as I could get it. He relaxed his jaws as he let out a horrific scream. I turned my finger to keep it lodged in his nasal passage and kept jamming it toward whatever he might have for a brain.

I wanted to probe his soul - or pith him like a lab rat.

My opponent was hollering differently - in a much higher octave now.

We writhed our way out from under the vehicle and I kept pounding the devil out of the guy that started this bizarre altercation. Now I had his range and was delivering jabs and crosses to his head. My fists were getting sore.

His face was a bloody mess, the sight of which pleased me immensely.

He went into a purely defensive mode and was no longer trying to hit me, so I stopped pummeling him.

"Now, you idiot, tell me why you wanted to kill me? I'm tired of providing entertainment to the whole town," I growled at him.

His two buddies said that he'd had enough. The guy was bleeding a lot, primarily from his nose, one ala or nostril of which appeared torn, as they led him toward a pickup with a federal government logo.

"Maybe you'd better put a tourniquet on his neck to stop that bleeding. Which of you jerks grabbed me?" I demanded.

The three strangers got in the government truck and drove away without further words.

My mechanic friend and some others from town came to me and suggested we all go back in for another beer.

No police, local or State Troopers arrived, which was about like things ought to be.

Well, after a scene like that, I pretty well had to go back in the bar to show that I was able to get around and was not too badly hurt.

But I was marked up and I did hurt. I had a cut lip and a puffy eye that would be black before morning. My ribs hurt and my left knee was aching.

So I asked if anybody knew who the guy was. All anyone offered was that he had flown into town in a Cessna 185 on floats. He was believed to be from Anchorage and had come to hunt moose.

My friend Larry said that he'd heard the guy bad mouthing guides. Someone said he worked for the state.

Bars were never a big attraction to me, even before this bizarre evening, so after one more beer, I went home.

In the morning, I looked a mess. The area all around my left eye was swollen and colored up, but I could see well enough. I had a cut lip. My left knee was stiff and I generally felt like I had been put through a rock crusher and spit out.

But, I did not let on to anyone that I felt so bad.

My guest hunter, Dave, looked questioningly at me, so I told him the story, minus how much I hurt. I was frying up some bacon and eggs to go with the coffee when the phone rang.

It was Leon Shellabarger, calling me from the hanger. I flew commercially for Leon and more than that, we were good friends, He asked me to come down for a cup of coffee before I headed up to the hunting camp.

So I took Dave along. I noticed that Leon, too, had a fat lip. Leon had been engaged in fisticuffs at the same time as my bout. He had been peacefully drinking, hunched over at the bar when a local guy came up, greeted him and accepted a drink on Leon. Then as Leon lifted his glass the ungrateful local slammed the heel of his hand onto the back of Leon's head, driving Leon's head onto the rim of the glass and the top of the bar.

So outside they went. The local guy was taller, younger and with a much longer reach than Leon. He was landing punches fast and regular on Leon's nose and head.

Leon got ahold of one of his attacker's arms and, in a clutch, forced him next to one of the piling cooling ventilators. (Solid pipes with cooling vanes -thin plates - extending about six inches from the shaft, similar to those on an air cooled engine.) At the ventilator Leon gripped the attackers head and drove it repeatedly into the cooling vanes until the local had a series of parallel cuts on the back of his head, all bleeding profusely. That ended their altercation.

"Jake, when you're my age, ya gotta end your fights quick, before you loose compression," he told me. Leon frequently came up with gems of advice like that.

So, I learned that the entertainment on the streets of Kotzebue had been a double feature the night before. We had been within a few yards of each other doing our own thing in our separate battles, but I was down and dirty in the mud, and had not been aware of Leon and his opponent. I was totally occupied with my own problems.

The hunt begins

As we could not hunt that day anyway, I checked the mail, answered the inevitable questions from folks who saw me, some of whom had heard about the fight. I took my time getting ready for our trip.

Dave was a snoose chewer. Big time. He used Copenhagen Wintergreen and he would place about a quarter of a can under his lip - a copious quid - each time he refreshed his chew. The size of his quid was enough to deform his facial features. On the flight to camp I was nauseated by the powerful smell of his tobacco. I chewed Skoal, but in small quids. This guy was something else! He was careful to spit into a little can that he carried. His mini-spittoon included a snap on lid and Dave never spilled any, but the pungent smell was still nearly overpowering.

I slipped the side window partially open to dilute the noxious stink inside the aircraft and hopefully clear my head.

Our ninety minute flight was unremarkable, with the exception of the smell of Dave's chew. About four o'clock in the afternoon I landed and taxied to the tie down spot. As I was helping Dave deplane, Mae came down to greet us and was visibly taken aback. My black eye and other scuff marks and abrasions, along with Dave's fat lower lip and his quiet manner gave Mae the impression that we had been in a serious fight.

"What's that smell?" she inquired, as soon as Dave was out of earshot. I explained that Dave had a serious snoose habit.

On a positive note, the fragrance emanating from Dave made him easy to locate without calling. I wondered if the Copenhagen might serve as an effective mosquito repellant, but there weren't enough of the pestiferous insects around that late in the summer to make a good evaluation.

Our Labrador, Zeke, seemed to keep his distance from Dave, probably due to the pungent smell.

Mae and Zeke in the main room.

We got Dave's gear, our food and supplies packed up to the cabin and installed him in the upstairs bedroom. Dave was a very considerate, courteous man. He suggested that Mae and I should take the upstairs bedroom which had more privacy, but we declined his offer. Mae preferred to be close to her kitchen facilities - the Coleman stove.

As a supper of baked Chum salmon, macaroni and cheese with a salad was in progress, I helped Dave sight in his rifle. Though his gun case showed signs of being battered, apparently the airline baggage handlers' abuse of his gun case, did not harm the weapon or optics, for it shot accurately without adjustment of its Weaver scope.

We were into the first week of September, well past the time when we should be seeing large bull Moose coming up the creek, looking for love or failing in that, a fight.

The tundra had taken on its technicolor autumn hues, cottonwood leaves were changing from green to gold, and some willows were turning yellow while the alders retained their deep forest green. It was all very beautiful, but the vegetation was still in its full leaf phase, seriously compromising our visibility in the dense patches So far this season we had not sighted any worthy trophies near the cabin, so after two days of glassing, with my aches and pains diminishing, I decided to take Dave in the cub to scout around. I had a good tent and was prepared for two or three days away.

Zeke, our Labrador, was disappointed to be left behind.

The Moose

When I got into my seat, I got a whiff of the Wintergreen and uttered a silent prayer that we would not have to fly too long before setting up camp. I have a strong stomach, but this was testing my limits. Nausea was a possibility.

Within fifteen minutes we found three large bull moose, but they were twelve miles down Trail Creek from the camp. I expected they would not come close to the cabin for up to a week. I decided to look over a good drainage to the east. After the July high water, the Kaluktavik River presented good gravel bars for landing a cub. We found several good Moose near the main channel. The animals were too close to the best landing bars to discretely land and set up the tent camp, so I flew a mile upstream before landing to make camp for the night.

Large Arctic Char were within steps of our camp site.

Most leaves of the cottonwoods in this area had already turned their beautiful golden color and before landing I could see plenty of large Char in the clear stream.

Dave expressed his wish that he had purchased a fishing license and brought some gear. However, I had the book of licenses and some metal locking tags along, for just such a situation, or perhaps a Caribou. I always carried a small fishing rod in the aft baggage compartment and, of course, some lures were in my survival package.

It took only a few minutes to have my guest properly licensed for the day. He worried that he did not have the ten dollars for the license. I told him we could take care of that later. This guy was conscientious to a fault.

Dave insisted that he help me set up the four man draw tight tent before he made the first cast, so I indulged him.

Gathering some dead wood for a small fire took only a few minutes As I went about preparing the fire place, Dave began waving his hands, motioning me over. He had beached a nice twenty-six inch, bright sea-run Char and wanted to know if that would be enough. I assured him that would be plenty for us to eat, but he could continue to catch more if he wished to do so. I replaced the Mepps lure he was using with one that had only a single, barbless hook and with his next fish, showed him how to release it with minimal handling, stress and damage to the fish. He continued to catch nice Char with every third or fourth cast, all of which were over twenty inches in length. He soon said he was getting tired of pulling fish in. It was the best trout fishing he had ever experienced, he told me.

The fish filets were seasoned with lemon-pepper, placed on my small wire grill and cooked on the coals for about fifteen minutes. I simultaneously toasted some bread and we were ready to eat. When he noticed the creamy top surface of the filets, Dave asked what I had basted them with. I explained that these fat fish, fresh from the sea, had so much oil in them that no basting or sauce was necessary … and they were delicious, as always.

I brewed a can of cowboy coffee and put it into a thermos bottle to avoid having to make a fire in the morning. There was no wind at the time, but the thermos gave us some insurance against a morning fire alerting the Moose.

The sun set about nine o'clock that evening and we slept well. I'm not certain that Dave's Wintergreen flavored exhalations anesthetized me to sleep, but I did drop off into unconscious bliss very quickly. I was still plenty sore from my pugilistic endeavors in town.

Dave was up to drain his bladder several times. The last time, I noticed that it was about six o'clock, so we enjoyed the coffee along with some store-bought bear claw pastry and set off walking down stream.

Haste makes waste and we had no need of hasty action at the moment. We eased down stream through the cottonwoods and willows. Within twenty minutes I heard a cow Moose's mournful call. Soon I could hear Moose antlers raking brush to our left. We'd seen several large bulls in the area just hours before, so I wanted to gain as thorough a perspective regarding what was available as possible.

Luckily there was no wind, otherwise I would have been anxious that Dave's Wintergreen would have alerted every animal and insect for miles around to our presence.

We stood in place. The brush was thick enough that we might suddenly be in close proximity to a taker bull. I whispered to Dave to chamber a round and keep the safety engaged.

The bulls briefly locked up.

The cow moaned again. Her call was quickly answered by the explosive grunt or a bull. Then we heard another bull a bit further away. We slowly moved toward where we reckoned the cow to be standing.

The sound of the clash of two sets of bull antlers was unmistakable. The animals were rattling their racks rapidly. It sounded like they may have engaged and locked antlers. We moved more rapidly in their direction. The racket coming from just in front of us would surely drown out our sounds.

I recall that I got a whiff of rutty bull moose and was surprised that comparatively delightful odor somehow dominated the Wintergreen miasma that enveloped us.

At sixty yards we could see the backs of the giant bulls and occasionally the tips of their racks. Their heads were down below their shoulders as they pushed and twisted their heads. In the confusion of racks and points I could not be sure which was the better bull. I placed my index finger to my lips, indicating the need for silence to Dave.

My dilemma was solved when a third bull came rushing in from our left side. When that bull was within ten yards of the engaged pair, he stopped and began to display his impressive rack, turning his head in wide, slow sweeps from left to right. There could be no better display of a rack.

He was clearly a taker, so I motioned to Dave, giving him thumbs up. Dave flipped his safety off, took aim and fired his .308 Norma magnum. The 180 grain bullet stunned the massive animal, but he stayed on his feet.

"Shoot him again, Dave," I told my guest.

The second slug caught the bull just in front of the shoulder which resulted in the hind legs folding and the bull falling over backward. I should have had a movie camera running for that spectacular sight. It is typical of how moose collapse after massive internal bleeding.

With all this disturbance a cow came running by us from right to left, only fifty yards away. She quickly disappeared in the willows.

The two fighting bulls seemed reluctant to disengage, but they did separate and look our way. Neither had as impressive a rack as the one lying on the ground.

They squared off again and clashed their antlers one more time before backing off and charging away in opposite directions.

In less than sixty seconds the scene and the world had changed dramatically. A profound silence settled in.

Dave's bull was not moving. The second slug had bored into the spinal column and put his lights out permanently.

We approached the fallen giant and Dave seemed stunned at the size of the beast. After probing the back of the carcass with my rifle barrel, I walked to the head and probed an eye. The bull did not react to either test.

It's eyes were both open in a vacant stare. He was stone dead.

Dave sat down on the withers of the great bull and began to sob quietly. I had seen this reaction in hunters before and I understood.

I gently patted Dave's shoulder and told him I knew how he felt.

A special sadness comes with taking the life of such a magnificent animal. Weeping in such a situation is reverent - respectful of the life of another occupant of this amazing world, to which we all belong.

I would much rather see this sort of reaction than have the hunter whoop a cry of victory.

A few guest hunters have wanted to immediately measure the width of the antlers or measure the overall score of game they have just taken. I refuse to do that. No such measurements will be made in my camp until well after the animal has been dispatched and butchered.

Once the animal has been taken, no matter what the numerical score, it is done and that's that. The trophy had better be good enough, because the final commitment has been made.

The hunter and his quarry are wed, for better or worse.

We made a few photographs and went about taking the big animal apart. Dave did not wish to have a shoulder mount made, much to my relief.

A moose cape, necessary for a shoulder mount, weighs about eighty-five pounds and a mount takes up a lot of room, as well as costing several hundred dollars in taxidermy fees and freight. If a cape is taken, nine full man loads instead of eight large loads are required to pack it out. Additionally, moose antlers are better displayed flat on a wall, in the European tradition.

This moose was lying on its right side, so to begin, I removed the left front leg, leaving the skin attached. Then I removed the left hind leg with skin on. The skin would be removed just prior to packing the meat out. I cut down the midline of the back from the base of the antlers to the rump. The topside back strap was carefully cut free of the carcass from the base of the skull to the pelvis. This skinless strip of prime meat and neck was about eight feet in length and weighed about sixty pounds. I draped it over a nearby willow bush and together, Dave and I rolled the carcass over to allow the same procedure to be followed on the right side.

Once the four legs and two back straps were removed, I opened the belly, allowing the guts to partially spill out. It takes only about twenty minutes to dismember a moose by this method and is so much easier if one is not slipping and sliding in a huge pile of warm guts. I cut the diaphragm free and used my Hudson Bay ax to chop the ribs from the back bone and sternum. That chopping is much easier with someone pulling back on the ribs. The heart was cut free and placed upside down to drain before I carefully dissected the tenderloins from their interior attachments. Each tenderloin weighed between seven and eight pounds - prime eating, especially if bacon is added. I placed them on a patch of clean moss.

The skull was cut free with my knife at the foramen magnum. Finally, what remained of the carcass was again turned over to allow me to chop out the ribs on the right side. I did not normally recover the liver.

Only fifty yards from the river, I walked over to check the gravel bar and found it was one of the best ones for landing the super cub. I left Dave to remove the hide from the head as I walked back to strike the camp and fly the cub down to the bar.

With each of us packing four large loads, we had the meat and rack ready to load into the cub in short order.

I tied the head on the right wing struts and placed the back straps, tenderloins, and heart on a tarp behind the passenger seat.

I always avoided getting any blood inside the airplane as it is difficult to clean out and even residual smells would be attractive to bears.

Dave's sleeping bag and gear were loaded on top of the meat.

After double checking to see that our chambers were empty and our magazines were full, I cranked the cub and we flew off to the cabin.

Since the shooting I had not noticed the odor of Wintergreen, but Dave stuffed a generous quid under his lip for the trip back. I countered his action by leaving the left window half open.

With another trip yet to make to recover the bulk of the meat, the tent, and other camp gear I flew directly to Trail Creek.

As we flew over, Mae was on the hillside picking blue berries for pie. She did not expect us back so soon. Zeke was zeroed in on the airplane and ran down to meet us. We quickly off loaded the meat and antlers and I went back for the rest of the moose and camp gear.

When I landed near the kill site, only about an hour after departing with Dave, a gang of ravens was already pecking at the gut pile. On a hillside about a mile away I noticed a sow Grizzly with two cubs headed in my direction. They would soon be dining on our scraps. I always had my rifle close by on such chores, just in case. It took me less than fifteen minutes to load up and depart. The bears were still a quarter of a mile away when last I saw them.

With plenty of daylight left, Dave helped me pack the meat to the "A-frame" I used for hanging game and we were done well before supper time.

The delicious smell of fresh blue berry pie still a'baking was delightful beyond description.

Dave brought out a small bottle of Kentucky Bourbon with which we toasted the great Moose and our exceptionally fine days in the Arctic wilderness.

After a fine supper of fresh moose meat, baked potatoes, salad - and blueberry pie, we sat outside on lawn chairs and again toasted the day and life in general.

It is great to have no noisy neighbors or traffic on an occasion like this.

How lucky we felt to be able to see and enjoy this pristine, wild country. We gave our heartfelt thanks to God.

Mae had fun razzing me about my black eye which I had almost forgotten.

The Grizzly

We arose early the following morning and enjoyed our first cup of coffee on the roof, from where we took turns glassing the valley for game. I hoisted the chairs up, placing the legs astraddle the ridge line for stability.

Zeke always watched from below, looking like he wanted to be on the roof with us.

Dave spotted a blonde sow Grizzly with a single cub working through a large berry patch on the alluvial fan across the creek from us. They were nearly a mile away and oblivious to us, in spite of Dave's Wintergreen. Dall sheep were visible in all quadrants. We counted thirty-seven sheep, of which nine were legal rams. Dave told me that he would like to hunt a ram, but would save that for a future trip. He wanted a Grizzly first.

Mae announced that breakfast was ready, so we climbed down the ladder and enjoyed Spanish omelets, which were a step up from the store-bought pastry of the previous morning.

We were blessed with another nice day with a ten mile per hour wind drifting down the valley from the North. It's always best to hunt into the wind, so Dave, Zeke, and I headed up the creek toward the North Overlook.

Sheep were everywhere, seeming to taunt us. I reminded Dave that he could pursue a ram simply by purchasing a metal locking tag, or using his Grizzly tag, then replacing it with another, but he insisted the Grizzly had to come first.

Old Murphy was playing with us, which has not been an infrequent occurrence in my life.

After an unhurried hike to the North Overlook, we sat down to have a sandwich. We'd seen a lot of fresh Wolf tracks in the mud near Current Creek and one set of Wolverine prints, but got no sight of the manufacturers of the tracks. Zeke's reaction - the hair on his back stood up, indicated that some of the Wolf tracks were fresh.

With the ideal conditions of the day, we went on an extra three miles to Seagull Pass and took a look into that drainage. That was a fortuitous decision as we came upon a band of sixty-three Caribou, including two good bulls bringing up the rear.

Few American hunters are not impressed with Caribou. The racks are so much larger than those of Mule or Whitetail deer, all the bulls look really big. I could see that Dave was leaning toward shooting one, but the difference in price of a Caribou tag and that of a Grizzly bear was about a hundred dollars. Dave said he would hold off on the Caribou. Oh well, it would have been an eight mile pack, not that bad for two people, but chances were good that we would find a Caribou closer to the cabin … maybe even, after he got his bear.

A solid overcast moved in from the south and we began to feel a spit of rain as we made the trip back to the cabin.

The grade up and down Trail Creek is hardly noticeable, until time to go home. We may have been glassing less as well, but our trip back took much less time than going out. We arrived shortly before dark and smelled the supper. Along with the meal, Mae told us that around mid day, she had glassed a single bear on the slopes above Popple Creek.

The next morning came with a soaking rain. I climbed up on the roof to look around and saw a dozen cow and calf Caribou on the runway before my binoculars became too wet to be of much use.

We lazed around through that rainy day, reading, napping and snacking. Zeke frequently looked askance at me. He didn't mind being out in the rain.

Dave said he was hoping to loose some weight. I'm often heard that from guest hunters. I reminded him that we ran a hunting camp, not a fat farm.

Day six began with a dense fog, obscuring even the willows in the yard. By ten o'clock the sun was showing through in places and before noon we had a clear sky.

We three and Zeke walked up on the East slope, Mae to pick berries with her rifle slung, while Dave and I glassed for bear. We concentrated on the area around Popple Creek where Mae had sighted the bruin two days before … and there it was. Browsing around on an open hillside, slurping up berries, no doubt.

About four miles separated us from the bear. This was some of the most disagreeable walking in the valley, full of waist high pucker brush that had few trails, complicated with muskeg swamps that in places went over the tops of hip boots.

But Dave wanted to try for that bear, so off we went. Zeke happily accompanied us. The first three miles were conducive to rapid walking, especially along the gravel bars of Trail Creek. Tracks of Grizzlies, Wolves, Caribou and Moose were abundant, so we exercised caution lest we spook another potential trophy as we headed for the one on the hillside.

We arrived at the targeted hillside in about ninety minutes, but the bear was nowhere in sight. It was time to sit down and scrutinize our surroundings.

Time seemed to drag.

We saw a huge flock of Willow Ptarmigan winging down the valley. There must have been over three thousand birds flying in a tight formation. That time of year such large congregations move off the North Slope and head for more southerly climes in which to spend the winter. Some flocks are so dense they appear to be a small aircraft.

I told Dave that we should plan to get some Ptarmigan one evening at the cabin, as they are top quality table fare.

Then I saw the top of the back of the bear as it moved along slightly below the ridge line of a swale just ahead of us. First I would catch a glimpse of the dark line of hair, then it would disappear. Dave never did see it. There were enough contours in the hill to hide the bear for extended periods. I told him we needed to get over there right away.

With Zeke at my left heel we hustled through the tundra tussocks and eased up over a low ridge. Just before topping out I whispered to Dave to turn away from the bear to muffle the noise, and put a shell up the spout. He quietly shoved a round into the chamber.

There, about a hundred yards away was the Grizzly with its head down and feeding. Its butt was the only target. A "Texas heart shot" is fine, but I prefer bears to be hit the first time in the shoulder, if possible. I gave Dave the clenched fist hold sign to wait until he had a broadside shot.

Zeke saw the Grizzly too, and leaned into my left leg. I patted him and whispered, "Quiet."

Mixed Bag Hunt

Dave getting ready for the second shot.

It was a dandy boar.

When the bear turned a little to its right, offering a quartering broadside, Dave looked at me and I nodded affirmatively. He dropped to his knee and squeezed the trigger. The bear dropped to the tundra, then rose and tried to bite its flank. The shot had struck it a bit aft, but had disabled the hind legs.

The bear came up on its front legs, its hind quarters still on the ground. It grabbed at the tundra in front of it, in an effort to come our way.

"Shoot him again," was my standard comment in such situations.

Dave's second shot into the chest dropped the bruin for good.

We approached the bear from slightly uphill. I jabbed it in the back with my rifle barrel. Seeing no sign of life I walked to the head of the bear and saw that both eyes were open in a vacant stare. It was a dead bear .. and a mature boar.

Zeke was standing off, wary, until I told him it's okay, at which time he moved in and jammed his nose into the bear's belly. He was showing us what a fearless dog he was! He seemed to be indicating that he was tougher than the Grizzly.

We had plenty of daylight left and the temperature had risen into the high forties, so skinning was done carefully to minimize excess fat on the hide and weight to carry.

Dave, enthusiastic as always, dobbed a huge new quid of Copenhagen in his mouth and volunteered to carry either the hide or the meat. So, I let him pack out the two hinds. This was a sweet bear, having been feeding on berries and roots, it would provide some fine roasts and gravy.

We three were back to the cabin before dark.

My left eye was still black, but beginning to resolve. I hadn't looked in a mirror all week and was surprised by my appearance when I did. It seemed I had mustard on my face.

Dave surprised us when he brought out another bottle of his prime Kentucky squeezin's. He was a frugal man, but had his priorities and was pleased to share with us.

The Caribou

The aroma of Mae's biscuits and gravy woke me up. The coffee pot was full and I called to Dave to come down and join us.

Zeke got a generous portion of biscuits and gravy to top off his dog food and scraps.

The day was beautiful and before we had finished our breakfast I heard Ptarmigan clucking in the yard. A large flock had come in that morning and Zeke assisted Dave and I in harvesting a dozen of the plump birds. Two of the wing shot Ptarmigan hit the ground running. Zeke spent several minutes retrieving each of them, but when he handed them to me, both birds were alive.

That was indeed a fine dog we had.

With only two days left before he had to head back to Ohio, Dave was debating going after a ram, but he said that he wanted to save something back for the future. He told me this was the best hunt he had ever had and doubted it could ever be equaled, but he was willing to try and wanted to book a hunt for 1980 before he departed.

Mae had gone back up the hill to get more berries. She wanted to bake us a Crow Berry Crisp dessert and have some fresh cranberry sauce to go with the Ptarmigan dinner. She always took her rifle and binoculars on any trip from the cabin. Zeke went with her.

We could have left the birds to skin after dark, but Dave wanted to do them right away, so we skinned and butchered them, saving the gizzards, hearts and livers and placed the breast pieces and legs in a Teriyaki marinade to soak for the day.

Preoccupied with the bird butchery, I had not kept track of Mae's meanderings. When I did look up and see her, she was waving for us to come. I told Dave that judging by the rapidity of her waves, we'd better get up there pretty quick.

I had the presence of mind to put Dave's Big Game Tag record and a metal locking tag for both Caribou and Dall sheep in my pack.

We burned plenty of extra calories going up that hill. When we reached Mae, we were sweaty and out of breath. She said that several Caribou, all bulls, were just over the skyline in East Bowl canyon. She said one of the bulls looked really good.

We peered over the crest of the hill and observed the bulls, some lying, while others fed on the hillside just beyond a small stand of willows about four hundred yards up the canyon.

Pulling my paperwork and the tag out, I asked Dave if he wanted to buy a tag. He nodded in the affirmative. The paperwork was completed in about two minutes.

I motioned to Zeke to lie down and he crawled along on his belly as we hunched over and began to get higher on the hill.

Most animals are less apt to look up hill than in other directions, so we moved up a shallow draw to position us higher than the Caribou.

We had no decent cover, so in the exposed places we lined up to make only one silhouette for the bulls, and we moved very slowly.

There were nine bulls in this bunch and they all seemed relaxed and unaware of the danger that was inching closer with each step we took.

But nine pairs of eyes, especially those of adult open country critters are not apt to miss the approach of predators for long. I was pleased that we'd managed to come within two hundred fifty yards of the band of Caribou when one of the bulls, a young one, threw up his head and stared directly at us.

We froze. I whispered to Dave to chamber a round.

He asked the range. I told him to figure on three hundred yards, but to not hold higher than the top of the animal's back. (Most shooters hold too high and shoot over the animal.) I told him to wait until I told him to shoot. Then I asked if he had the best one picked out. We agreed that it was on the far side of the group and highest on the hill. It was obviously the best, but it's always a good idea to be sure the hunter has the same critter in sight and mind.

The alerted youngster remained transfixed on us for several minutes. Then, it turned downhill and went back to feeding.

If the animals buggered, they would most likely run further back into the canyon and shooting an animal on the run, surrounded by others, would be a challenge. I told Dave that he should set up with a comfortable rest and make his shot from where we were. He agreed.

Dave was a very methodical person and he adjusted his pack with his coat on top several times. I could see that he was stressed. He took several deep breaths, then he stopped breathing and squeezed the shot off.

The bull dropped straight down on all four legs and was still. The other eight animals startled, then confused, ran a few steps down the valley, turned, stopped, and ran up the valley for a hundred yards before stopping to look back at their fallen companion. Again, I should have had my movie camera, but it was on the table in the cabin.

We all stood up and walked to the Caribou as the rest of the band watched. This bull was a dandy with nine long points on the tops of the antlers, good bez points and a decent shovel. Clearly he was wearing the best antlers in the group. The rack was so impressive Dave wanted to take the cape for a shoulder mount.

So, after caping the trophy, I butchered it following the same pattern as we used on the Moose. Had it not been for the cape, I would have gutted it then come up two ribs from the last and cut it in half for taking to the cabin to hang in two pieces.

Mae packing out Dave's caribou head and cape.

We were back at the cabin by one o'clock for lunch.

Dave, in spite of his reserved personality, was ecstatic that afternoon. He told us that he had heard of so many hunts in Alaska in which the guest hunter had been totally skunked. In the last few days he had taken fine trophies of the three animals he most desired and planned to add a Dall ram the next year.

Our evening meal was composed of fried Ptarmigan, chicken fried Caribou, baked potatoes, fresh wild cranberry sauce and Crow Berry crisp.

Jake, Zeke and Dave with his three trophies of 1979.

Dave bought another one day fishing license and spent his last day with us catching and releasing Arctic Char and Grayling. He handed Mae a two hundred dollar tip for the extra fine cooking and Caribou spotting and gave me five hundred dollars for a deposit on his hunt for a ram in August of 1980. And he praised Zeke's performance.

And my black eye was fading from the color of mustard.

1980 The Dall Ram

In late September of 1979 I got a chance to charter a single engine DeHaviland Otter to fly building materials from Kotzebue to Trail Creek. I had intended to get the stuff up sooner, but the materials had been purchased in Seattle and shipped up by barge. The barge was late, so it looked like I would not be able to move the freight until the following summer. A week or so after Dave departed I happened upon the owner of the freight outfit, Buck Maxson, who told me he could do the job if I got the material to him at the airport. He'd made a trip like that to Trail Creek in 1978 and knew the strip, so I set about getting the several tons of lumber, plywood, insulation, etc. to Buck's place at the airport.

It took three full Otter loads ($600 per trip) to haul all the stuff, including two Honda 110 ATCs, to Trail Creek. Despite some problems, including one Otter wreck by one of Buck's seasonal pilots, we got it all in and secured for the winter.

As soon as the aufis glacier retreated enough to give me sufficient runway to land the cub, I was back up with a older fellow who turned out to be a really fine bush cabin builder and a trusted friend. His name was Ray, and we two set to putting the two story lodge together. In five weeks of long days spent cutting wood and pounding nails, in spite of the worst mosquito season I have ever witnessed, we had the new building ready for use.

Dave arrived on August 8 and was the first official guest hunter to stay in our brand new lodge.

Having been at Trail Creek for practically the entire summer, I had as good a notion as possible on where the Dall sheep were and had been. It seemed that all the mature rams we'd been watching had vacated the main Trail Creek valley during the first week of August. I do not believe that our sometimes noisy activity in constructing the lodge had any negative influence on the sheep. They just moved, perhaps in search of greener pastures.

The tourist season was in full swing in Kotzebue, with Wien Airlines bringing from dozens to scores of visitors on daily and overnight excursions. Mae wanted to be at our little store, Arctic Rivers Trading Company, to make the best of the increase in tourist traffic, so she deferred coming to the lodge until September. Ray stayed on with me at Trail Creek to do some finishing work and help with our guest hunters. Ray spent several evenings catching Grayling and Char with his fly rod and home tied flies. He caught and released 57 grayling in one three-hour period.

Dave practically skipped down the jet's stairs and greeted me with a hearty handshake and a broad smile on the airport tarmack. I was expecting my head to be knocked back by his essence of Wintergreen, but did not detect the distinctive aroma. I noticed that his lip was not so protruding as before. The large quid had given him the appearance of having a Class Three malocclusion, but today he looked normal.

As we headed for home after retrieving his baggage (home was one half block from the terminal) I asked him if he had quit the snoose habit.

"Jake, my wife had been after me for over twenty years to quit the Copenhagen, but I ignored her. Then last winter I got a touch of pneumonia. The doctor read me the riot act for using snoose, especially in such large amounts. I was forbidden from dipping while in the hospital, which irritated me, but after a week without the tobacco, I no longer liked the taste of the stuff. So, I just quit, I guess," was his explanation.

After congratulating him I told him that he was more handsome without the big lip, he looked younger, too.

"Yeah, you look a little better without the black eye and scuffed up face, too. Had any good fights lately?" he countered.

"Nope, I've remained pugilism free, so far, since last I saw you. I didn't like the prolonged healing time," I told him.

We stopped by the store, where Dave greeted Mae and purchased some trinkets for his grandkids and a nice ivory necklace for his wife.

Again, Dave brought good weather with him. We stopped briefly at Hanson Trading Company for some vegetables and fruit which was not prime, but it was as fresh as we could find, and loaded the cub for the flight to Trail Creek.

This time I chose the direct route, through the Baird Mountains, to give my guest a different view. As we flew by Tutulatak Mountain, about midway between Kotzebue and the lodge, I saw several sheep in the bowl. From a distance I could tell that they were rams, so I banked and flew by at lower elevation to look them over more closely.

One of the rams was a heavily broomed battler that was the best ram I had seen for a couple of years. I descended to check out a marginal strip that I had used once in 1976. The dog legged bank of an old stream was grown over with knee high pucker brush and had a bit less than six hundred feet of usable length. Steep canyon walls rose up from about fifty yards on both sides. Landing could only be done going up creek and slightly up hill. Take off would have to be down stream and down hill. It demanded a minimal load for safety. Had I not been there before I would have had a hard time detecting this potential access to the bowl that held the big ram.

With the plan to enjoy the comforts of the new lodge dominating my thoughts, this impressive ram demanded a fresh evaluation. I asked Dave if he felt up to a tent camp and a long walk for a chance at that exceptional trophy.

"Anything you suggest is fine with me, Jake. If we're not going to have Mae's fine cooking anyway, we may as well rough it," was his response.

Ray was expecting us with the fresh food, we were too heavy for the strip, and not prepared for a tent hunt, so I flew on to Trail Creek.

We had that day and the next to spend before sheep season opened on August 10.

Ray had a heart condition and although I had taken him for a sheep for himself the year before, he told me that he felt he should not participate in sheep hunts with guests, so he was fine with us going for the Baird ram. Zeke, however, would be disappointed, as he would have to remain with Ray.

We had a good supper of aged Caribou steaks from a cow that we'd taken a week earlier, baked potato, and salad topped off with pie and ice cream that had to all be eaten before it melted.

In the morning I collected our gear for the two to four day tent hunt. When we were ready, Dave and I helped Ray with some minor projects, then cranked the cub and flew back to Mount Tutulatak.

As we departed Trail Creek I noticed some sheep on the Southwest aspect of West Bowl, but did not check them out at closer range.

We flew high over the bowl that held the sheep. The five rams were still in place. I expected them to remain there for our attempt the next morning

A breeze of about fifteen miles per hour was coming down the creek at the brushy bush strip. That would be good for our landing. A slight cross wind component was not enough to cause us grief. I made one low level pass with full flaps, the strip looked okay and the plane felt right, so I banked right and committed the machine to a full stop landing.

As we approached the threshold I told Dave to hold the cross brace above his head and prepare for a bump or two. I put the main wheels into the pucker brush just where I planned, touched the ground, bounced two feet in the air and came down again, stopping quickly. The brush served to restrain us, similar to a tail hook employed by aircraft landing on a carrier. Considering all, it was a smooth landing. I chopped the throttle and we deplaned.

Before taxiing to the upper end of the strip we used my ax and saw to cut brush to avoid mowing it down with the propeller. I was using a Borer prop for high performance, but the blades on that propeller are longer and thinner - not designed to be used as a hedge trimmer. Once the strip was cleared I moved the cub to the upper threshold and tied it down to the tough willow brush. Then we trimmed more brush on the down creek half of the strip.

Mosquitos pestered us as we set up the tent. Deep Woods Off is a potent insect repellent and serves as a good male deodorant as well. The malevolent blood suckers were effectively stymied in their attempts to drain us of our vital fluids.

With thirty minutes of easy work we had the four man tent set up and a fire pit ready. We were far enough from the sheep that I discounted any chance of a small wood fire alerting them.

First thing in the morning we were up, dressed, poured starting fluid (coffee) down our throats, gobbled some oatmeal and pastries, placed our lunches in my pack and we were off to see the wizard - in this case, the big ram.

We followed the main stream up toward Tutulatak for two hours, noticing lots of beautiful stream polished fossil rocks beneath our feet. Most of the fossils were coral heads, cone shells, and other occupants of an ancient warm sea bed. Continental drift - the movement of tectonic plates - had thrust them up to this elevation, about three thousand feet above the current sea level. A geologist I had worked with a few years before told me that the organisms whose skeletons were incorporated into the fossils we saw were alive one to two hundred million years ago. Many of the fossils we encountered were of museum quality. I placed a few of the more outstanding ones in my pack, but Dave deferred, saying that the sheep would be enough weight for him to carry.

When we reached the base of Tutulatak we left the east bound creek and turned north. The climbing at first was relatively gentle, over tundra. As we gained altitude the moss, sedges and lichens were interspersed with more and more rocks and the incline became more abrupt.

Fossilized coral heads.

Our progress slowed due to the steep terrane, coupled with our increasing vigilance for sheep. A steep ridge of bare rocks and chimney chutes separated us from the bowl that held the sheep, but thinking that one or more of the rams might top out above, spot us and take the whole bunch to parts unknown kept me on edge. Sheep do that, sometimes. We proceeded slowly, watching above with each step.

By mid afternoon we were near the crest. For the past hour we had been trying to avoid dislodging rocks, but in spite of our caution, several boulders had rolled and bounced their way down the mountain. Such sounds do not normally spook sheep as loose rocks commonly come clattering their way down the slopes.

At the jagged crest I eased over to look below, expecting to see the five rams, but the basin was devoid of white spots. I motioned for Dave to join me.

Disappointing as it was, our best bet was to remain in place and continue to carefully dissect the terrane with our binoculars. Perhaps a fold in the land, an unseen swale, or depression still harbored the rams.

But no. There were no sheep in the basin. I had no idea why or to where the sheep vacated that fine meadow.

This was not the first time such an event had baffled me, nor would it be the last. No aircraft had flown over that day, nothing had occurred to our knowledge that would explain the disappearance of the sheep.

Perhaps this was a band of *Ovis disappearicus*, a common type of sheep sub-species familiar to most sheep hunters.

We were skunked, for the moment. We had been snake bit, one might say.

After spending an hour on the crest and seeing no sign of sheep, we turned back down the chimney chute and trudged back to camp, stopping frequently to glass the surrounding country for sign of the rams. We located only a single cow Caribou, nothing more.

As we returned to the camp, I loaded two medium sized fossil rocks that I had placed on prominent features along the creek, into my pack. Dave picked up a small fossil to use as a paperweight back home. Treasures like those are well worth the effort to pack out.

Arriving at the tent about ten o'clock that evening, we had two more hours of full sunlight. I heated some water and we ate Mountain House meals and crawled into our bags.

The next morning we walked back up the creek and climbed the mountain to the south of Tutulatak. I noticed mountain Dryas and other favored sheep fodder was more sparse on this side and after spending the day, we sighted no sheep and not much sign. Where had those rams gone?

It was time to return to the lodge. With nearly twenty-four hour light, and favorable flying conditions, we quickly struck the camp.

I walked the strip over again, then satisfied, I gave the engine a good warm up until the cylinder head temperature was above one hundred degrees and the oil temperature gauge indicated sixty. Holding the brakes I pushed in full throttle, then released the brakes and the cub sluggishly began to roll. I kept the tail low for maximum lift angle of the wings, then just before the far threshold I raised the tail a little to gain a bit of speed. At the far end I popped on full flaps and we jumped into the air, but began to settle, so I pushed the stick forward which gave us enough more airspeed to avoid a stall. We staggered down the creek clipping some of the taller willows with the tips of the propeller as we gained airspeed. A projection of the hill on the right required a hard turn to the left, so I lowered the nose some and we barely cleared the obstructions. We slowly gained airspeed and altitude. After forty-five minutes of what became an uneventful flight we landed at Trail Creek.

I inspected the super cub's horizontal stabilizers and found that a willow had ripped a three inch hole in the fabric on the left side. I had repair materials in the cabin, so I put a patch on that evening.

Zeke anxiously came to greet us. Its always uplifting to experience the unconditional love of a dog or a good friend.

Ray hadn't seen any sheep from the lodge, but he had not concentrated on glassing, he just kept working at building furniture, shelves and so forth.

Rain pelted the building and clouds hung low on the mountains the next morning. It was not a good day to be in the high country looking for sheep preoccupied with avoiding a dangerous fall on the slick rocks. But fish don't care about the rain, so Zeke and I took Dave down the creek where he caught some nice Char, one of which we kept for supper. A ten dollar license is not much to pay for that kind of enjoyment and first class eating.

Conditions began to improve the following day, but drifting clouds kept the sheep country intermittently obscured, so we hunted Ptarmigan.

The birds had not yet come in great flocks from the North Slope but local coveys were sufficient to keep us occupied. We took a dozen birds, some of which were used for supper and the left overs were set aside for lunch.

The best bet for us when the clouds cleared the next day was to walk up into West Bowl where I had seen some sheep five days before. So we set off in that direction, with Zeke at my heel. I planned a day trip, with us returning that same evening.

We scanned West Bowl but found no sheep. A fresh trail led up one of the chimneys to the jagged crest, so we followed that. Across the ridge we saw nothing so began to walk to the north. At each new vista we sat and put the binoculars to good use, but found nothing until after five o'clock that afternoon. Three rams were well below us feeding near a rock outcrop closer to the bottom of the range and the head of Popple creek than to the higher country where I expected to find them.

If we connected with a ram down there, we would not make it back to the cabin before night. Attempting to traverse the mountain in poor light is seldom a good idea. The sky was overcast, promising a dark night. But sheep were proving difficult for us, so we bailed off the ridge and went for the lower promontory. An hour and a half had us within five hundred yards of the still feeding rams, but there was no cover between us and a location within decent range for a shot. We waited another hour until the rams fed lower and went out of sight.

We managed to get within two hundred yards of the sheep. One of the rams was slightly broomed on one horn, but had more than a full curl on the other. It was an "argali" style rack, curling close to the chin, then turning out. It was the best ram of the group in my estimation. But Dave wanted the second best ram which showed both intact horn tips and was wider. I told him that would be fine.

Shadows were lengthening as the sun sank lower in the west, when the rams turned and began to feed back up toward our position. I told Dave to chamber a round, set the safety, and wait for my signal to shoot. If lucky, he would have a shot at one hundred yards or less.

The light was fading as the rams slowly came our way. Dave wanted to shoot, but I told him to hold a bit longer. He was just above me and to my

Me, still deaf, and Dave with his ram.

right when he fired. I had not heard him slip the safety off. The muzzle blast deafened me, but I saw the ram tumble.

I looked at Dave and must have appeared to be angry, which, indeed I was. My ear throbbed and was ringing.

"Jake, I should have told you, but I knew you would say to wait. I was afraid I would loose my chance, so I shot," he said pleadingly.

Thinking there was nothing to be gained by detailing my ire, I resisted telling him that my ear was blown out, at least for the time being, and he should never discharge a gun so close to another person without a warning. He should not have shot without telling me.

The ram was the one he wanted and a decent trophy. Zeke was elated, of course. We did a quick couple of photographs and set to caping the sheep. I was hoping to get at least to the crest of the range before having to siwash camp for the night.

My under cloths were sweaty and I knew they would make me super chilled that night, so I stripped and took them off. I advised Dave to do the same, but he declined. We loaded the meat into my pack and Dave took the head and cape, but there was no way we would make the top of the range before full darkness.

As we labored up the mountain I saw a ledge which formed a cave-like shelter which would be welcome if the darkening clouds dumped more rain that night. We needed to go only a little out of our way to reach that cave as it began to drizzle.

We jammed ourselves up into the little cavern. I took the sheep cape and placed it on the rocks with hair side up, then placed a space blanket over the make shift mattress for Dave to rest on. For myself and Zeke, I used a space blanket. Dave and I each ate our last sandwich. I shared mine with Zeke. We wolfed down a candy bar, had a swallow of water and tried to sleep. Soon after settling in we were cold. Mountains in the Arctic are like that. Even in the warmest time of August, if one is caught out, the ground cold will chill the warmest blooded men. Zeke curled up in front of my belly and was like a heat blanket for me, but Dave began to shake. I suggested again that he remove his wet t-shirt and shorts, but he would not do so. I believe Zeke is the only member of our group that slept at all that night, but I may have lost consciousness for a few brief moments.

The drizzle turned to light rain and continued for about two hours before the overcast began to break up and a few stars appeared. I could hear Dave's teeth chattering and felt his involuntary shaking throughout the prolonged night.

When I emerged from our shelter about five o'clock I started to stand, but nearly fell down. The act of moving had pumped cold blood from my extremities to my body core and I felt more cold than ever.

I've noticed on other occasions that after sitting for some time in a cold situation, even though I was not feeling chilled, when I rose up to walk, my being seemed to be flooded with cold and my motions were erratic.

When Dave rolled out I cautioned him to be careful about standing up. He attempted to rise, but fell immediately to his knees.

Our core body temperatures must have been significantly lowered by our unusual night out on the ground.

We each devoured a candy bar and began to slowly walk toward the crest of the mountain. I gave Zeke a piece of dried whitefish that I found in my pack. After twenty minutes or so of walking we had adequate control of our legs and were feeling much better.

Our trip back to the lodge was deliberately slow, taking extra precautions to not fall or twist an ankle or knee. We arrived about four o'clock in the afternoon and were completely spent.

It had been a real sheep hunt, all right.

Seeing our condition, Ray hung the meat up and prepared supper, which included barbecued sheep ribs, though curiously enough, neither Dave nor I felt particularly hungry. We did eat some ribs though.

Dave produced a bottle of fine bourbon and after a double on ice which Ray had chipped from the aufis glacier at the end of the runway, we both gratefully went to bed about seven o'clock.

I have no recollection of anything until after eight the next morning. Dave was still snoring, but Ray had coffee and sheep tenderloins with friend eggs and home made sourdough bread ready for us all.

Ray offered to remove the cape from the head of the sheep, turn the ears and split the lips and eyelids, but I told him I would do that. His carpenter talents were better used on wood work.

Dave was not due to depart Kotzebue until the evening flight of the next day, so we had plenty of time to kick back and recover from our ordeal of the day before.

When I delivered Dave to the Wien desk he shook my hand and told me that he would never forget that hunt.

I assured him that I would remember it as well.

Dave gave me a Lifetime Membership in the North American Hunting Club and I enjoyed the benefits of that organization and its magazines for many years.

1980–1982
Ulrich and Heiner

Polar bear hunting began in the 1950s and brought guides from all over Alaska to Kotzebue and other sites in northwest Alaska. Most polar bear hunts were done using two aircraft. I recall counting thirty-eight small aircraft from super cubs to Cessna 180s tied up on the ice in front of Kotzebue in early March of 1970.

When snow conditions and weather were favorable, after the polar bear was taken, many of the hunters would pursue wolves, wolverine and inland grizzly bears in April and May. A permit could easily be obtained to legally shoot wolves from an aircraft and many did so. It was forbidden to take grizzly bears on the same day one was airborne, but many guides ignored that restriction during the first fifteen to twenty years after statehood. Few arrests were made.

The secrets of many previously unknown remote regions of Alaska were incidentally revealed to those who came north to hunt the ice bear. And they remembered.

Passage of the Marine Mammals Protection Act in 1972 brought a sudden end to polar bear hunting by any but coastal dwelling Alaska

Many pairs of polar bear hunting aircraft converged on Kotzebue from February to April.

Natives. But some guides continued to come to northwest Alaska with its many inland grizzlies, wolves and wolverine - and few game wardens.

Two of the worst outlaw guides focused on spring grizzly bears, but took wolves, wolverine and whatever else they could manage in Game Management Unit 23. They headquartered in Kotzebue and used two super cubs and sometimes a Cessna 185, which served as the "mother ship."

These fellows were experienced hunters. But even more important to their illegal activities, they were excellent pilots, operating at the edge of the envelope - sometimes beyond the edge. They wrecked and used up an average of one airplane per year.

The Alaska Department of Fish and Game was aware of the illegal harvest being conducted by primarily that one pair of bandit guides, but try as they might, they could not make an arrest. There was no game warden (Protection Officer) stationed permanently in Kotzebue until 1976.

Since state game managers could not reign in the depredations of those two pirate guides, or catch them, in 1980 the State made a drawing permit mandatory for anyone hunting grizzlies in Game Management Unit 23. This was a major inconvenience to honest guides and it had some unintended consequences, the worst of which was the huge increase in the number of grizzlies. The once healthy moose population was steadily reduced. Most of the cows dropped twins, but their newborn calves were quickly eaten by grizzlies. By August, most cow moose were without calves.

The drawing for grizzly permits was in place until 2019 - for 39 years. When the drawing requirement ended, the State allowed grizzly hunts to begin on August 1, instead of September 1. Early August skins are seldom prime enough to go through tanning. Also, beginning in 2019, residents of Game Management Unit 23 could take two grizzlies each year. Previously an individual could harvest one grizzly or brown bear once every four years. For several years now, any hunter, resident, non-resident or alien could take one grizzly every year. The moose population still declines.

The State had no idea how many bears had been taken illegally by those outlaws. In 1986 at a show in Houston, I was standing next to the former Commissioner of the Department of Fish and Game when one of the pirate guides approached me and asked if we could "work out a deal" to allow him to hunt moose in one of my areas. I knew this rascal and would not deal with him, but I was not offensive about how I told him, so he kept talking. He was very good at piloting and a few other things, but his downfall was that he enjoyed running his mouth and indulging his self importance to all.

During our conversation the former Commissioner asked the guide how many grizzlies he and his partner were taking in the Kotzebue area. The department figured it to be about sixty each spring. The guide laughed and told him that they never took less than a hundred grizzlies every spring! About three years later I was working in northern Australia - the Top End - for Bob Penfold. Someone brought a copy of the Alaska Magazine to camp. In it was a story about how that same guide had been prosecuted and given several years in federal prison for his game violations. One of his "clients" was an undercover agent who befriended the guide, who then allowed him to video several violations. Additionally, dozens of his clients had their illegally taken animals removed from the record books.

So, anyway, in 1980 we had to make applications for permits for anyone wanting to hunt a grizzly bear. I was fortunate that two of my booked guests received grizzly permits.

In late August I greeted two German men, Heiner and Ulrich, at Alaska Airlines in Kotzebue. Ulrich would become one of my best, life-long friends. In the next forty years, he would come to Alaska to hunt and fish more than a dozen times. And he encouraged me to hunt on his property and the forest areas he managed near the Elba River.

So this was the first year to use our new two-story lodge. Ray remained to assist, my wife Mae came up to assist and cook, and my nine month old labrador, Max, assisted also.

Weather was cool and clear. Heiner told us that he never was rained on - anywhere.

On opening day of grizzly season, September 1, we spotted a large grizzly pawing and gnawing its way through the berry patch off the end of the runway. As usual, the wind was blowing down the valley so I took Heiner and Ulrich to the northern edge fo the willows that lined South Bowl Creek to put us downwind of the bear. Max was with me. After waiting thirty minutes, Mae and Ray began walking from the lodge toward South Bowl Creek. The bear winded them and began a brisk walk toward the

Ulrich is 6'2." His shot was perfect and the bear fell with a broken neck.

place the Germans and I waited. Heiner insisted that Ulrich be the first to shoot, since he was a few months older. The bear came to us as if to a beacon.

As soon as Max was certain that the bear was dead, he began poking his nose aggressively into the belly of the beast. Yeah, Max was showing us he was one tough dog, as his predecessor Zeke had done.

We celebrated with a bottle of fine wine that Ulrich provided. That evening we counted more than forty sheep from the lodge windows and we watched moose walk up and down the valley, looking for love. But we saw few caribou.

The next day was another beautiful one, so I took Heiner and gear for a tent camp in search of caribou or grizzlies. Less than five miles down stream from the lodge I found a large grizzly atop a pile of debris which partially covered a large moose carcass. Part of one antler showed. We returned to the lodge and made plans to visit the kill site the next morning.

We were on the cutback overlooking the kill site by mid-morning. The bear was sound asleep near the mound of tundra covering the moose.

I whispered to Heiner to put a round in the chamber, place another round in to fill the magazine and get ready to shoot.

Heiner said he didn't want to shoot a sleeping bear, so I whistled and the bear stood up. Immediately Heiner fired and the bear dropped.

This was a mature boar - a bit larger than Ulrich's bear.

We removed tundra to expose both antlers of the moose.

Heiner wanted to take the moose antlers to Germany with him, but I told him that would require that he buy a non-resident tag, which was $300. He did not want to do that, but without a tag, shipping the fresh antlers would be too controversial and would surely invite close scrutiny by protection officers. If I were a game cop I certainly would be looking to seize the antlers. So, I carried the rack to the lodge where Ulrich cleaned and bleached the skull before mounting it in the main room, where it hangs today, forty-two years later.

We enjoyed hunting willow ptarmigan which were coming down the valley in huge flocks of hundreds or thousands. The migrating flocks of white birds had the appearance of low flying aircraft.

But the beautiful days were passing and we had yet to locate decent caribou for our guests. Ulrich and I loaded up and headed to town where I would switch to the float plane and we would look over the Selawik River country as fall migrating caribou frequently pass that way as they move to their winter grounds.

Max was in ecstasy during this, his first fall hunting trip to the lodge.

We found thousands of caribou in large herds. The animals were moving steadily, but not rushed. I found a pleasant little lake to camp. Ulrich and I enjoyed his nice homemade pear schnapps. As I dozed off I could hear the clicking of the feet of the passing caribou. When I awoke, the sounds were still cadencing from all around us. We were completely surrounded by migrating caribou. A light drizzle softened the sounds. The tent was drawn tight by extra cords and remained dry inside.

With so many large animas so close, we forgot to have a cup of coffee. Great herds command full and undivided attention. I would have been content to spend the entire day observing the many sets of antlers being displayed, but after two hours we had not seen any racks of outstanding quality, so Ulrich settled on two mature bulls with balanced head gear and all the components of normal racks.

We had to pack the meat one hundred yards to the tent.

It looked like a hard rain was coming from the southeast, so we struck the camp and headed back to Kotzebue. Days were still long, and we had time to fly back up to Trail Creek, landing just at dark.

The next morning opened clear and calm. Just after lunch I loaded Heiner and his gear and we flew to Kotzebue. Soon after landing we were in the float plane headed for the area I had taken Ulrich.

The overcast was dark and threatening, but we flew on. Heiner assured me that he never got rained on. I thought, "Right."

The caribou were still parading through in large numbers. This time I chose a larger lake in the flats. We quickly set up the tent, glassed many bulls and soon thereafter were in our sleeping bags.

Early the next morning I was awakened by the clicking of caribou feet, mixed with light rain. I nudged Heiner and we were both soon dressed and out of the tent. As we stood next to the tent Heiner pointed out that only my side of the tent was wet. His was dry. He side never got rained on. I might become a believer!

We glassed a bull with tall antlers and long, delicate points on the top of the main beams. Heiner wanted that one. We had to travel about a half

This is an attractive head, but it lacks development in the bez and shovel.

Nevertheless, it is an impressive trophy.

mile before a reasonable shot came available. Heiner carefully squeezed and the bull dropped as if pole-axed. But immediately the animal was up and running. I had seen this before. Either the bullet had struck the spinous processes of the neck or an antler had been hit.

Heiner shot several times, but did not connect. Much of the time the wounded bull was mixed in with other animals, making a shot inadvisable.

But after nearly a mile of pursuit, a clear shot was offered and Heiner's bull was on the ground to stay.

We returned to the tent about mid-afternoon. We struck the camp and loaded for the trip to Kotzebue. Once underway we encountered rain showers, which I mentioned to Heiner, but he said he felt no drops, so his record stood.

It rained hard in Kotzebue that night, but we were snug in my little sod house, dining on fresh caribou back straps and my Gallo wine.

There was only one day left on their booking, so Heiner said he would volunteer to stay in town and clean the skulls of his and Ulrich's caribou.

I loaded the cub with stove oil and as much other useful materials as possible for the otherwise empty trip to the lodge. A hundred pounds of salt and some 2X4 lumber topped off the load.

Ulrich, Jake, Heiner with Max and Ray with the September trophies.

We made time for a multiple species photograph. Mae had taken a Dall ram just before the Germans arrived. The two moose were taken by family members for meat in August. The valley had provided generously for us.

Ulrich's departure the next afternoon was sad for us all. He would return in just two years and then many more times in the next forty seasons.

1982 Ulrich's second visit

In 1982 Ulrich came back alone. This is unusual for most European guests, who much prefer to travel with friends. He joined us at the lodge along with two pleasant men from Florida - another Bob and Ray team.

Bob and Ray had come a few days earlier, so I should relate their experiences of the previous week or so.

This had been an especially busy summer. Along with charter flying in my super cub on wheels, my cub on floats, and Shellabarger's Cessna 180 on floats, I had framed and roofed in two major additions to our home. A thirty-two foot by twenty foot addition to the main floor would house a two chair dental clinic and small lab. The other addition was the most complex of the nine additions I had put on the original house. This was a second story thirty-six by forty-four foot single room on top of the existing main portion of the house. To avoid the inconvenience of having the house temporarily left without a roof, we added a pony wall, then build right over the existing roof. We got the two additions framed, enclosed and roofed with steel in less than one week with a framing crew of three men I flew up from Seattle. These men were competitive carpenters who did contract work for my friend and frequent hunting guest Bruce Moe. People in Kotzebue were amazed at the speed and efficiency of this crew, as was I.

I've always enjoyed telling stories that catch listeners unaware, getting them to ask a question that leads to my punch line. One of the framers, Kenny, had been suckered in on several of my better efforts and in frustration he bet me a hundred dollars that he would not be suckered again. This was a challenge I could not ignore.

At breakfast one morning I began to prepare my victim with stories of how government dentists, newly graduated from school, frequently called me for help with dental diagnosis or treatments.

On the morning of my friendly coup I had my wife call our home number from the phone in my clinic. I answered the phone in the living room so my guests could hear my reply.

"Yes, I get the picture. It's an easy solution," I responded. "Okay, I will jump in the truck and be right up. Relax, he's not going to die!"

Without further explanation, other than muttering that these new dentists had so little common sense, I left, returning after twenty minutes.

Upon my return, several of the crew asked what that was all about.

I explained that a local ivory carver, who was also a notorious drunk, had been bumming drinks at the local pool hall and after being pushed away by irate patrons, he picked up one of the pool balls and offered to put it in his mouth if they would indulge him with a drink. This fellow had a large mouth with no teeth, as I had removed them all the year before.

Irritated, one of the pool players used the heel of his hand to pop the ball into the carver's mouth.

The carver gagged, gasped and struggled to dislodge the pool ball, but it did not come out!

The folks in the pool hall became panicky that the man would suffocate, so they rushed him to the Indian Service hospital, whereupon the dentist also panicked and called me.

So amidst personnel in the emergency room, among whom were the dentist, a physician and a scrub nurse, with the carver still gagging and gasping, with tears coming from his eyes and face the color of raw liver, I showed them how to remove the ball. It was so simple.

All but my wife, who knew the story, gave me their rapt attention.

Kenny couldn't help himself. "How did you get it out, so simply?" he asked. Immediately thereafter, Kenny said "No, no…"

To which I replied, "Gotcha Kenny!"

I told him I took the choking carver back to the pool table, bent him over the edge, grabbed a pool stick, stuck it up his hind end and shot it out.

After the uproar, Kenny reached into his pocket and counted out five twenty dollar bills for me. I felt wonderful!

So began another productive day on my house building.

My first guest hunters of the year arrived on August 7. I was tired from the construction endeavors and looking forward to relaxing on some sheep pursuits.

On August 8 I started off to the lodge with Ray, but found some dandy rams on a branch of the Eli River, half way to the lodge. The cub was too heavy for the pucker brush strip so I flew to the lodge, unloaded and took Ray back to the Eli where I set up the four-man tent. Then I returned to Kotzebue for Bob. Sheep season opened August 10 so we spent the ninth looking over several rams and doing some Char fishing.

We headed up the mountain before daylight on August 10 and by mid-morning were within five hundred yards of three good rams when a super cub flew over, banked and buzzed the sheep. Those rams lit out for parts unknown. I did not recognize the cub and it had small numbers which I could not make out. I was angry. I never did learn who the cub driver was, but another local said he had a similar experience with the bothersome super cub.

We returned to the tent and the next day I flew the two men to the lodge. My Dad, sister Pat, and Max, my labrador were happy to see us.

The next day it rained hard, bringing the creeks all up and making the main river too deep to cross in hip boots. We enjoyed the comforts of the dry building, the library books, and Pat's good cooking.

The next day as the overcast weakened and visibility improved my Dad spotted two rams on Middle Mountain just to the east of the lodge. At nine o'clock we struck off with lunches in our packs and water in our jugs. The ascent to the crest of Middle Mountain was steep but not treacherous and we were walking the ridge within an hour. Bob was a bit bowlegged, so I asked him if he had been a cowboy. No, he had been a NASA engineer, the legs were due to a fight with rickets as child. Soon we found ourselves directly above the feeding rams at about two hundred yards. I told the hunters to get ready, but before anyone was ready one of the men fired accidentally. The rams were up and running over the ridge and quickly out of sight. I was sure they had not seen or smelled us.

In no rush we crossed a large cleft in the mountainside and by incredibly good luck we saw the rams once again feeding about five hundred yards from us. We crept along, stealthy as burglars, until we were within three hundred yards. We could go no further without spooking the sheep. Both men shot simultaneously this time and Ray's ram rolled down the hill, but Bob's sheep ran directly away with blood showing on its shoulder. Bob and I went as quickly as we could to see where his sheep had gone and saw it walking slowly uphill and away from us. We were able to reduce the shooting distance to a couple hundred yards when Bob hit it again. After a couple more approaches and hits, the ram finally toppled.

Bob and I are pleased with his ram.

We snapped some quick photos before beginning to work on Bob's ram. Of course I took the cape for a shoulder mount. Despite being shot four times, there was little meat loss.

We had about a mile to go back to reach Ray and his critter.

Both rams were nine years old and in robust condition. We wasted no time getting loaded up and headed back down the

mountain in the dark. I carried the meat of both animals and my guests brought out the heads and capes.

Loaded heavy as our packs were, we did not rush back to the lodge. There was more hunting to do and wrenched knees or ankles were to be avoided. We stayed on the ridge as long as possible to minimize our travel down the boulder and willow brush strewn creek bottom. We took plenty of short breaks -actually a couple of short naps - and walked into the lodge yard after two o'clock the next afternoon. It had been long, but very productive hunt.

My best friend from West Germany, Ulrich, was due in Kotzebue the next day, so I flew in to meet him and took most of the sheep meat to my freezer. Wild sheep meat is unsurpassed on the plate.

Ulrich arrived about eleven o'clock and was anxious to get to the lodge as soon as he could, so we loaded up and went north. I meandered a bit with Ulo as he so marveled at the wilderness. We flew up the Eli valley where I'd spent a couple nights with the other hunters, then jogged a bit east of the direct route to view the little Kaluktavik River, a beautiful drainage which I sometimes camped on.

We landed and as soon as I climbed out of the cub, here came Max, overflowing with excitement and love. My Dad had kept him in the lodge until he heard the engine shut down. It would be tragic for an enthusiastic dog to run up and be struck by the propeller.

We had a fine dinner of wild sheep tenderloins, the finest of all wild game meat in most people's view. My Dad had spotted a band of three rams in a particularly nasty canyon across the river and a bit north of the lodge which we called the South Bastards - because it was a real bastard to walk in, but there were good rams in it this day. Those rams were lying on the deepest spine at the head of the valley. If they were there the following day we would have a challenge approaching them, but it was worth the effort, as my "long eye" spotting scope confirmed they were all over a full curl.

At first light - about five o'clock - I confirmed the rams were still at rest on the nasty spine, so Ulrich and I struck off. Bob & Ray each already had their ram and were completely at ease with Ulrich attempting to collect

The South Bastards is the rugged canyon just under the snowy ridge. The dark object at nearly mid picture on the far left is my aircraft, tied down.

one. The four at the lodge would scan continuously for moose, caribou, wolves and whatever else might be moving.

We started out at eight o'clock. Ulrich is ten years my senior, but he is very fit and determined. Due to the lay of the landscape I took us deeper into the canyon by an up and down route just below the skyline. We would be in direct line of sight of the rams for much of our approach, but sheep - and many other big game species - seldom look up.

We went slowly, trying to not dislodge any large boulders from their tenuous positions in the broken scree filled slopes. On one small patch of mountain dryas and forbs we found several small grasshoppers. Ulrich put two in his pocket to investigate at the lodge. It seemed unlikely that we would find grasshoppers in such a place, but I had done so before in sheep habitat, however not in the lower elevations. There were never many.

We rested in some rocks across a deep gully and about two hundred yards from the rams. After about two hours a ram stood up and was soon joined by the others. The oldest of the rams mounted one of the others. It was a show of dominance and the younger ram seemed humiliated.

Ulrich assembled his Ferlach Drilling in .300 Winchester Magnum below double barrels of three inch magnum twelve gage shotgun. He snapped his Zeiss scope in place, settled on the oldest ram and fired.

The ram reared up and fell over backward. It rolled a short distance before coming to rest near a large rock. It was a dandy ram with both horns evenly boomed.

The other rams, alerted by the noise and the fall of their companion turned and began to walk up a particularly rough chimney and were soon out of sight.

Ulrich sat with his "widder" (German for ram) for some time. He admired everything about this old ram and told me he had not expected to take such a capital animal.

Ulrich is pleased with his old ram to which he as given the "last bite."

We did not make haste loading our packs and heading out of the treacherous canyon. We were back at the lodge by nine o'clock - just in time for a big meal.

Those at the lodge had seen parts of our stalk and the fall of the ram, but they did not hear the shot. They had spend most of the day scoping two single grizzly bears as the bruins coursed through berry patches.

I was feeling less tired now, after three sheep hunts, than I felt when we began the season. It must be the good water and the mountain air.

The Floridians were on a fifteen day booking and had yet to secure their moose and caribou. I decided to take one man in the cub in search of caribou. Since Rai shot the first ram, he suggested that Bob be the first to go in the cub. We took off about noon.

We found several impressive bull moose about eight miles downstream from the lodge, but that's much too far to consider packing. The bulls would move upstream as the season progressed, but we needed to shoot soon, so I flew over to the main Kuguroruk River where we found lots of moose with a high percentage of bulls. I found a great place to camp about a mile from a willow and cottonwood patch that held a dozen moose, three of which carried capital racks.

We could not shoot until after spending a night, so we set up the tent, got out a fishing pole and Bob landed one Arctic Char of about eight pounds - a perfect supper for us. The night was cool and calm and we were serenaded by wolves on several occasions before sunup. The lobos were no doubt hunting, too.

Breakfast was the usual for trips like this - store bought Bear Claws and thermos bottle coffee. Mixed with the excitement and anticipation of taking a superb trophy, it always seemed adequate.

We had only about a quarter of a mile to stalk through the riparian growth before a dandy bull came in sight. We crept through the undergrowth to within eighty yards and Bob put the big bull on the ground with one shot.

Immediately after Bob's shot the brush erupted with moose. I counted eleven animals tall enough to be seen over the underbrush, of which three were mature bulls, but Bob's rack was the most impressive - that was sheer luck. It's antlers were in full velvet, but the tips of the points were all hard, making it within days of beginning to shed the velvet.

This moose is sixty-five inches in width with pleasing, symmetrical antlers.

We had an easy pack back to the tent. It took four loads each and we were ready to head back to the lodge by mid afternoon. I would return in the cub for the bulk of the meat.

When we arrived at the lodge I saw my Dad and Rai carrying moose meat from the alluvial fan directly across the river from the buildings. That was their second trip.

That morning Dad had spotted a big bull wandering across the fan so he and my sister, Pat, who held a Registered Guide license, took Rai directly to it, but, by law, moose did not require a guides assistance.

The bull had come close to the cutback that runs along that side of the river and was standing on the edge, apparently contemplating descent into the heavier bush alongside the river. Rai's shot decided things for the moose and it tumbled straight to the bottom.

At the base of most cutbacks like this runs a well used game trail. This was the case here and the trail showed not only heavy moose traffic, but

the recent rains had made mud that held the paw prints of a large grizzly, So the moose was butchered by Dad and Rai with Pat standing guard.

When I returned with the rest of Bob's meat I made one trip helping pack Rai's meat.

Daily we saw a handful of cow and calf caribou, but it was mid August and the herds were not coming off the north slope in my area. I took Rai for a trip to the Utukok River about thirty-five miles north of the lodge, but we found only scattered cows with calves and several grizzly bears, but no impressive bull caribou. I flew east to No Luck Lake, found it to be well named and so full of water from heavy snow melt that no beaches offered a place to land on wheels.

The following day I took Bob north west to the Iliglurok River, then to the Kokolik River. We took a lunch break on a gravel bar of the Kokolik, found some small bits of mammoth ivory and some interesting fossils, but no trophy caribou. It was the same story. Wherever the mature bull caribou were, we were not! Never in the fifteen years I had been hunting this country had I seen so few caribou and such a total absence of big bulls.

All too soon we had run out of time! I flew first Bob, then Rai to Kotzebue. Bob made arrangements for them to have a car and a two day sightseeing layover in Anchorage. When I took Rai in, I diverted to the west and behind Cape Krusenstern we flew over a huge caribou with the

We made some photos of the collection of three guests.

most impressive set of head gear I had ever seen, but he was in the middle of a massive field of huge tussocks. No place to land - or even walk.

So it was not without my best efforts that we found no trophy caribou, but this was the first time I had sent guests home without one. I hoped it would be the last. I was very disappointed to see my fine friends from Florida depart without their caribou, but they remained in good cheer.

After seeing Bob and Rai off, I loaded up fresh fruit and vegetables and headed back north. Ulrich's time was running out, so I suggested we go back to town, then take the float plane in search of caribou or black bear.

Two years before Ulrich had enjoyed his first ride in a small seaplane and he was happy for a repeat performance. I purchased some pastries, cheese, crackers, sausage and little else before flying east to the head of the Selawik River, then we surveyed the foothills of the Sheklukshuk Range for black bears. The blueberry crop was splendid and the bears were out in force. We counted more than twenty black bears in two hours in one small area. I landed on a lake that had bears on all sides within a mile of us.

The sky was clear with nearly a full moon as we enjoyed a fine bottle of German wine, cheese, sausages, crackers and each other's company.

As the coals of our little fire dimmed, two maniacal loons tuned up and their serenade sent chills down my back. It was after dark and things were cooling down rapidly. It was time to zip ourselves into our sleeping bags.

We both realized how fortunate, or more appropriately - blessed - we were and we drifted off to sleep. We were serenely content.

We rose early the next morning amidst the silent, pristine wilderness. After some fresh cowboy coffee and pastries we were off to climb a nearby hill covered with blueberry and birch.

Our passage alarmed the resident squirrels which scolded us as we trespassed on their area. During one of the squirrel diatribes a black bear stood up about ninety yards uphill from us, then dropped quickly out of sight.

We reached the top of the slope and found a bench broken by copses of spruce trees and large, relatively flat expanses of willow, dwarf birch and blueberry bushes. I noticed a dark shadow intermittently appearing across a tussock patch from us. It was a foraging black bear, but as we approached, two more dark objects appeared near the first. The largest dark object was a sow and she had two small cubs.

Ulrich and I watched the family of bears for a few minutes but we moved on in hopes of finding a large single bear in a more visible locale. I had a Super 8mm movie camera and Ulrich had his 16mm film camera.

We did not find an ideal photography situation, but after five hours of interesting walking we had counted eleven black bears. Only two were large single bruins. Ulrich decided to harvest what appeared to be the largest bear we'd seen that day. I doubt any of these bears had ever been stalked by humans before this day.

With only knee high cover and full sunlight we stalked and crawled to within seventy yards of the bear, which was preoccupied with slurping up luscious ripe blueberries.

Ulrich's careful aim sent his bullet through both lungs and out the off side. The bear exploded and ran at top speed for the nearest line of spruce trees, but, drained of its vital juices, it collapsed about fifty yards from the spot it had been feeding.

As he had done with his Dall ram, Ulrich gave the bear its "last bite" by placing some blueberry stems in its mouth. Then he sat contemplatively

Ulrich's boar squared about six and a half feet.

admiring his harvest for some time. That is a nice German tradition which renders respect to the animal and causes one to more profoundly appreciate the entire experience.

"Waidmannsheil, Ulo," I said.

"Waidmanns dank," Ulo returned.

We skinned the bear carefully to minimize excess weight leaving the skull and paws in place for later removal. I laid the two rear legs aside to take with us. This bruin was so robust, I took the front legs, too. I tied strings around both ends of the stomach to preserve the recently picked contents. Many of the berries in a bear's stomach are not even broken and the contents always make fine pies. I tied off the gall bladder and kept it to give to an attorney friend who's oriental wife had faith in its medicinal power.

Our time allowed for another night in the tent, which to both of us, was preferable to a night in Kotzebue. Again we were entertained by the resident pair of loons and high above we saw the first string of lesser Canadian geese winging southward, which reminded me that within a couple of weeks the lakes and tundra would be ice covered and locked up for the winter.

The Narcoleptic Visitor

In 1983 we were joined in camp by two guest hunters from the East coast. These men had come through Kotzebue with a Wien Air Alaska tour group accompanied by their wives in early July that same year. When the group visited our little store, Arctic Rivers Trading Company which we'd recently expanded from 760 to 2208 square feet, they expressed interest in taking an evening flight seeing trip. We had a section of the store set up as sort of a little museum with emphasis on local trophy animals, along with remnants of Wooly Mammoths, Mastodons, Steppe Bison, fossils and other items of interest. The displays were a magnetic draw for tourists and in addition to bringing the visitors into the store, where many purchased mementos, a few of the people arranged for aircraft tours of the region, one man purchased a sixteen ton jade boulder from me - money from that paid for the store addition - and occasionally, I booked a guided fishing or hunting trip with a tourist from the group.

The Arctic can be quite chilly, even in the peak of summer with its continuous daylight and relatively hospitable weather. To counter the chill, as well as encourage tourists to get into the Eskimo frame of mind, Wien issued colorful loaner parkas to the passengers as they deplaned. As the groups of often rotund touristas moved slowly around town looking over the unique activities and sights, one of the local wits noticed their similarity to Easter Eggs and soon summer tourists who visited on tours by Wien Air Alaska were referred to as "Easter Eggs."

One afternoon I was doing some minor mechanical work on the float plane when I returned to the house in my greasy overalls to get a tool and a cup of coffee. A tour bus had just stopped in front of our store and disgorged its load of Easter Eggs. Two of the not so rotund eggs approached me and asked questions about life in the Arctic. One of the men was a Harvard professor named Bob and the other, Ray, was an inventor and manufacturer of small items from New Jersey. As their wives perused the store the men arranged for a flight tour for that evening. For single passengers I made the flights in either my super cub on floats or the one on wheels, but with any group, I needed to use one of the Shellabarger Flying Service planes, in this case the Cessna 180 on floats was available for that evening.

We flew for more than two hours, followed by a visit to our home and a glass of wine. The passengers were enthralled and told me that little trip was the highlight of their excursion to Alaska. The inventor, Ray, asked if I might have time in my booking schedule to take them big game hunting the very next month? I was pleased to tell them that I did have an opening during prime time in August. They gave me a deposit for a three week hunt for Black Bear, Moose, Dall Ram, Caribou and whatever else might come available. This turned out to be the best booking that I ever made as a direct result of the store and its mini-museum.

The Sheep Hunt

The pair of men arrived on August 8 and the next day i flew them to the lodge, one at a time in the super cub. My Dad, my sister, Pat, and our labrador, Max, were already at the lodge.

As we walked the hundred yards of so from the landing strip to the lodge, Ray asked what was the most wonderful aromatic odor he sensed. I told him it was Hudson Bay Tea and that we had some dried leaves of that plant with which to make a tasty brew. Nothing, it seemed, was lost on these two appreciative, observant gentlemen. They were as eager as kids on an Easter Egg hunt.

This pair of urbanites had an unquenchable thirst for wilderness pursuits and now, late in life, they were trying to satisfy their long deferred dreams. Ray was a youthful sixty-five and Bob was nearing sixty-three. They had been diligent in their businesses and finally decided that they were more apt to run out of time than money, therefore they should begin to do some of the most important things they had reluctantly sacrificed on their individual alters of success.

It seemed that nothing escaped their attention and appreciation. As I watched them fly fishing for grayling and Arctic char the first day at the lodge, I was reminded of small children catching their first fish. I always delight in seeing adults so enthralled by simple pleasures. The fish were fried that evening and made an extra course for the wild game supper Pat had ready when we returned.

Prior to their arrival I had thoroughly scouted the valley and knew the whereabouts of three bands of sheep that were within walking distance. Each group held at least two taker rams.

Our first morning began at four o'clock. We struck off for the sheep I deemed most liable to move away due to their normal meandering urges and their previous late summer movements.

Things could not have gone better for us. After two hours of walking at a comfortable pace, our binoculars revealed five sheep lazily grazing on a slope we could reach in only another hour and a half. The wind was light and variable and the sky was clear. Our only delay occurred when we stopped during the last of our ascent to allow the band of five rams to move behind a small ridge. Once the last of the sheep was out of sight we moved directly to the rock strewn outcropping and found ourselves within one hundred fifty yards of our intended quarry.

The sheep were in no rush as they ambled about, selecting the most tempting green groceries from their lush mountain garden.

We were in no hurry either. Bob and Ray had drawn straws, cut cards, knife fought, or by some means known only to themselves, decided that Bob, the Harvard professor, would be the first to shoot.

With such an ideal, unhurried situation it seemed prudent to take maximum advantage of our opportunity. I asked each man to remove his jacket and use it to make a soft rest to steady his rifle for the shot.

The rams all were legal, with horns of a full curl or more, so I told my guests to decide which one they preferred, however it would be a good idea for one man to shoot the ram farthest to the right and the other fellow take the ram on the extreme left. It would be an unnecessary shame if the hunters each shot the same sheep. The ram on the far right carried a noticeably heavier set of horns, so Bob selected that one.

Professor Bob and his fine ram.

The Narcoleptic Visitor

Before we heard the first echo of Bob's shot, Ray had dropped his ram as well. Ray's ram stayed in place, but Bob's struggled to rise, then fell down a rocky chute and was still. His shot had been just a bit forward of ideal and had exited at the throat. The ascending aorta had been completely severed. The ram became dizzy and expired quickly. There was virtually no meat loss from either ram.

As so often happens, the three remaining rams looked around, then went back to feeding. The mountains frequently shed loose rocks and the sound of gunfire is apparently mistaken for rolling rocks, but as long as the sheep have not seen or winded the hunters, they seldom spook.

We watched those magnificent animals for a quarter of an hour until my guest's could no longer suppress their urge to more closely inspect their trophies.

When we rose to our feet, the other rams startled, ran up over the nearest ridge line and were gone.

It wasn't even midday yet, so we took our time with photographs before caping the rams and butchering the carcasses. Wild sheep provide some of the finest meat imaginable and of course none was ever left behind.

Bob and Ray with their rams.

We loaded the heads and capes on Bob and Ray's packs and I stuffed all the meat in mine. With most of the three week booking in front of us, we descended carefully to avoid wrenched ankles and knees. As we made our way back, Ray commented that prior to the day with me and Bob in the chartered float plane he had never seen and seldom dreamed of a Dall ram, but from then on, he would often dream of his ram and would see it every day in his home. Bob added his ditto to the thoughts.

None the worse for wear we walked up the runway in plenty of time for Pat's big supper, topped off with fresh blueberry pie.

Each time we flushed ptarmigan, observed a lemming or heard the gurgling of the stream, these fellows, tired as they were, marveled at the wonder of the place and the events of the day.

It was a special reward for me to be accompanying such appreciative people.

The August caribou movement had slowed to a trickle and it was still early to be expecting moose up near the lodge. The bulls would begin wandering up in another week or so, looking for love in the form of cows in estrus.

Ray, Bob, my Dad, Pat and me with the first rams of the season.

Black Bears and Moose

It seemed best to take advantage of the superb weather by going back to Kotzebue, then taking a tent in the float plane to search for moose and black bears, both of which were commonly found that time of year in drainages to the southeast of town. As Bob had the first shot on sheep, it was Ray's turn to go first for the seaplane trip. The next morning we put the sheep meat in the freezer, spent part of the day in Kotzebue before departing about five in the afternoon for the moose pastures and black bear meadows.

Ideally we would take a bear before the moose as once the moose was down, I normally had a full day or more getting the meat to the plane and then to town and into the freezer or distributed to local family and friends.

That evening well before time to make camp we flew over a black bear sow with four cubs. I had never seen so many cubs with a black bear before and have not since.

Every day in true wilderness may produce a unique experience.

We set up the tent on a small lake surrounded by many other ponds. We had seen more than a dozen bears within three miles of our camping

Ray and his black bear boar.

site and most of them had been singles. It is illegal to take cubs or sows accompanied by cubs - a good regulation.

Weather continued to bless our efforts. We spent a cool, calm night with loons serenading us with their maniacal calls as we slipped off to sleep.

After cups of cowboy coffee and hot oatmeal we began stalking our way toward a nearby lake. By noon we had seen only three lone black bears and had turned them all down as they appeared too small. Black bears are harder to judge for size than the other species of bears and I have often erred on the side of caution, lest we harvest one too small or an immature animal. By mid afternoon I glassed a bear that looked suitable feeding on blue berries on a nearby hillside. We went directly to the animal where Ray, at about seventy yards, rolled it with one shot.

This bear had a single white spot below its throat. Such an interruption in the solid black pelage of *Ursus americanus* is common in bears taken in the south forty-eight, but I have seldom seen it in Alaskan black bears. Most Alaskan black bears are solid black. This older boar had well worn teeth and an estimated age of fifteen years.

We were back to the camp site in time to strike the tent and move on to look for a good bull moose.

After only twenty-five minutes in the air, we located several huge bulls within a mile of a decent sized lake, so I landed and set up camp again. Not wanting to alarm the moose, we did not fly low over them to inspect their racks closely, but clearly they were big.

I positioned the fresh bear skin over a bush to dry for the night.

Our sleep was undisturbed, save for quacking of ducks and the occasional splash of the tail of an offended beaver that happened to swim close to the airplane.

We awoke full of energy after more than eight hours of restorative slumber. I stirred first, quietly slipped into my britches, crawled out of the tent, and started the small fire. There was no wind. As the initial whisps of grey smoke from our fire rose into the nearby spruce tree I felt warmly caressed by the sun as its rays filtered through the foliage to reach my cheek.

We were blessed by another beautiful, calm, cloudless morning.

It was Sunday and we were in my favorite church, the exquisite, unspoiled cathedral of wild lands. The most pristine of chapels.

Together, speaking in hushed tones, we enjoyed a leisurely breakfast of store bought bear claw pastries, coffee and sausage before the first mosquitos reminded us of our goal for the day.

We were looking for a capital bull moose.

With some reluctance to depart such a idyllic setting , we donned our hip boots, slipped into our packs and headed for a slight distant rise in the terrane.

The young birch trees and broad leaf willows covering the gently sloping hillside had all been pruned off to just above eye level. Obviously they had been heavily browsed by moose. Moose pellets and droppings indicated that many of the big deer had been using the area all through the last winter. The less pelletized poop and hoof prints confirmed that numerous *Alces,alces gigas* had remained in this prime habitat well into the summer and were still around.

The dense growth forced us to proceed step by step, making as little noise as possible as we worked our way toward the higher ground. At times my nose confirmed the faint essence of moose. With visibility restricted to ten yards or less in many areas, I was concerned that we might stumble into a big bull and flush it away without an opportunity to appraise its rack, much less make the decision to take it, and then for Ray to get off an effective shot.

We continued at our pace, which seemed approximately equal to just a bit faster than that of a stealthy snail. We both walked with rifles at the ready. I whispered to Ray to stuff a shell into his chamber and set the safety as quietly as possible. My barrel remained empty, but ready to load.

A columns of midges spiraled upward from a slight clearing from which emanated the definite, strong odor of moose.

Dense thickets and diminished visibility of any kind have never been my preferred hunting areas, but early in the summer the moose remain in the dense areas as they go about their primary activities, which are making meat and growing antlers. We had to go to the jungles where the moose were hanging out.

We gained the top of the rise and I was surprised and relieved that we had not heard even one large animal go crashing away through the vegetation. With such an abundance of sign it was no less than amazing that we had not interrupted some of the great beasts in their peaceful hideout.

Physically the distance we had traveled was not worthy of heavy breathing, but we were exhausted and breathless from the tension and expectation of an abrupt confrontation with a giant moose.

From our newly attained high spot we had no improvement in visibility. The vast sea of young birch and willows stretched uninterrupted for more than a mile on every point of the compass.

It was time to stop and assess our situation. The lack of even a hint of a breeze was beneficial to our blind stalking, but brought with it the danger of any sound we made being carried to every ear in the vicinity. And moose have huge ears.

One of my rules is, if I don't know what to do, its better to do nothing, rather than act blindly. So we stood in place, listening more than looking.

Moose have large ears and use them effectively. For the situation in which we found ourselves, I was wishing that my own ears stood out even further from my head than they already did. I removed my cap, inviting even the slightest of sounds to penetrate to my auditory system.

Without a doubt, I could smell moose, but where was it, or they?

Trying so intently to pick up a noise, I thought I heard something, but told myself I was trying too hard. Then, again, I thought I heard a vague noise somewhere below us. I went to my knees and placed my right ear the to the ground. My attempt at picking up any ground sonar waves failed.

Ray had a quizzical look on his face when I stood up. I shook my head. I wasn't trying to play Indian.

Something was periodically making faint barely perceptible noises, but I kept hearing the sounds, for sure. It suggested a small object rubbing against a branch, but it was not the sound of a moose violently rubbing velvet from its antlers. It was much more discrete than that.

My mind raced through every imaginable possibility. Could it be a beaver gathering branches to take to his lake? Might it be only a snowshoe hare? We'd noticed a lot of pellets and seen two hares.

Placing my index finger to my lips, I signaled silence as Ray and I began to creep toward the source of the sounds.

We were covering not more than five or ten yards per minute but I wondered if Ray could hear my heart beating a full velocity tattoo.

The Narcoleptic Visitor

Less than seventy yards from the top of the rise I noticed what at first appeared to be some dark, bare branches surrounded by grass and small willows. I stopped and stared. Then I saw those bare branches move ever so slightly - but they moved in unison. I realized I was looking at the velvet covered points of a massive moose rack. I motioned to Ray who, rising to his tiptoes, was soon able to spot the object of my concentration. The moose was lying with its back to us, occasionally flicking its ears and moving its head to ward of the pestiferous whitesox (biting insects) that were bedeviling it.

Holding up my palm, I signaled to Ray to wait. I knew this had to be a big bull, but just how big was yet to be determined. We crept to within about thirty-five yards from the animal. In the dense brush, if it startled, jumped up and ran, there would be little time for a killing shot. Furthermore, Ray, who was a bit shorter than me, would have to maneuver to get a clear view of his target. Our position was good, but a bit less than perfect.

Using my binoculars I was able to detect points from both right and left antler and estimated the space between to be about six feet. If the rack was reasonably symmetrical, this was a whopper of a bull. With even close to a six foot spread, it was a certainly a shooter.

Ever so slowly I eased Ray up in front of me. I whispered that it was a taker and he should be ready to shoot, but only after I told him to do so. We took halting steps toward the lying bull. As we closed the short distance I kept expecting the giant to rise up and charge away. At twenty-five yards, I motioned to Ray to stop. We stood, waiting for something to happen.

The old bull continued its unsuspecting rest, ears flicking away the insects and occasionally moving its head slightly. Over coffee that morning I had explained to Ray the importance of shooting a moose in the neck, just behind the head, as a spine shot will drop them in place and damage almost no meat. The meat of this animal would be of of the highest quality at this time of year and I was expecting to pack it away for our family use the coming winter.

My heart rate had slowed to a hopefully inaudible rate, but Ray was getting antsy. Now we had most things in our favor. Ray would have an obstruction free shot when the moose stood up and should be able to stick a rifled missile right where he wanted it. We were still more than two hours on the morning side of midday. There was no need to rush.

Time flies, they say, but in a circumstance like the one we were in, time drags along interminably slow.

Finally the indolent beast stirred. Maybe he grew tired of resting. As he slowly came to his feet, he revealed his immense, symmetrical rack. Just as the great beast stood fully erect, Ray placed his 180 grain bullet about six inches behind the back of the skull and the moose dropped right back into his bed and never quivered.

Ray let out a whoop, looked at me, I nodded for him to go in front and after a few steps we were standing by the nose of the moose. For the first time we were able to fully appraise the entire enormous rack. The antlers were nearly perfectly symmetrical with points sprouting from the entire perimeter of the huge palms. Lying there in the grass and brush, he looked like he was supporting two sheets of plywood on his head.

The dark brown velvet had a few streaks of white and in no place was any of the antler fur (velvet) rubbed away from the bone. The antlers displayed a unique beauty that Ray said he would like to have preserved. I told him that was an unsure issue, as retaining velvet on racks was an iffy proposition, but I would do what I could to get them to the taxidermist of his choice with velvet intact and he could deal with the problem from there on.

Ray sitting aboard his outstanding moose.

Its always been my policy to never put a tape measure to any animal in the field, but I was more than just a little bit curious about the width of this extraordinary rack. I had figured it to span at least six feet, or seventy-two inches, but up close I felt I must have under estimated the beast. When we did put a tape to the antlers back in Kotzebue, it measured an astounding seventy-six and a half inches in width. This was the second widest moose rack I had been involved in taking, so far. The widest had spread over eighty inches, but it had not the palmation, points, or beauty of of this true giant.

To say that my guest, Ray was excited does not do justice to the breathtaking joy he felt at the moment. He told me that he wanted to have a full shoulder mount done and for this moose, I did not mind in the least tending to the eighty-five pound cape.

Once the cape was removed Ray and I set about dismembering the carcass by removing the left front and rear legs, leaving the skin on until we were ready to bone them out and put them into the plane. I boned out the top back strap to make an eight foot long strip of meat that ran from the base of the skull to the rump. We rolled the moose over and removed the legs and back strap on the right side, before I chopped out the ribs and carefully pared out the tenderloins. We saved the heart and liver, as Ray liked liver. Once again we rolled the carcass over to chop free the ribs on the left side. We had the moose ready to pack out in just over two hours after taking the last picture and one hour after finishing the caping ... and it wasn't quite noon yet.

The whitesox that had been feasting on the moose had moved on to us, so we kept moving and swatting. Liberal doses of repellent seemed to serve as no more than a spicy enticement to the molestacious bugs.

As we chewed and swallowed a sandwich I noticed the tops of some small cottonwoods just over a nearby rise, so I walked over to get a better look at our surroundings and found a long finger of water that led to another lake. The strip of water was too narrow to turn the floatplane with power, but we could taxi in and then turn the cub by hand. Once loaded, I could taxi out into a wider part of the new lake and take off. Using this lake would save us more than a mile of packing the meat and trophy. With the cape, we had a total of nine stagger-worthy loads to get to a lake shore, so reducing the distance by that mile translated into saving us several hours of hard work - while all the time being relentlessly aggravated and chewed upon by the ubiquitous airborne kamikaze insects. Our necks and wrists were already bleeding from multiple welts that rose from whitesox bites.

In two hours we had the meat, cape and antlers sitting on the bank of the narrow finger of water. Ray and I returned to our camp, struck the tent and landed on the new lake. In another forty minutes I had the back straps, tenderloins, heart and liver in the float compartments. I tied the antlers to the spreader bars of the floats and placed the moose cape and black bear hide and quarters in the cabin immediately behind Ray. It was a heavier than average load for the return trip to Kotzebue.

Making a slow taxi through the finger of water I noticed the stern of the floats was was submerged up to about eight inches in front of the water rudders, indicating a heavy load. On the wider part of the lake we had no problem getting on the step and soon were airborne and headed for town.

After the ninety minute flight I unloaded my passenger and freight, drove them to my home, refueled the cub, and was back in the air to pick up the bulk of that prime meat.

With most of the meat removed from the bones, I was able to fit it into heavy plastic bags in the float compartments which are located at the center of gravity of the floatplane. The rest I placed in the passenger seating area. The plane was prevented from becoming bloodied by the heavy plastic bags and blue tarps.

Its no good to have a bloody smelling airplane that may draw bears. Blood is extremely corrosive on aircraft tubing, as well.

When I arrived at home with the load of meat, my wife Mae had moose tenderloins already festooned with bacon strips and Ray had produced a bottle of fine red wine from his luggage. We enjoyed our filet mignon with a baked potato and wine before hitting our bags at nine o'clock.

We had seen only one moose that day, but that was all it took. We might have spent months ... or years searching for such a world beater and come up empty handed. One just never knows what might be beyond the next hill or behind the next bush. What a memorable day that had been!

The next day I dissected the moose meat by following fascial planes and placed pieces of meat in quart or gallon zip lock bags. I held each bag under water in the kitchen sink to express the air, then sealed them. I call it the "poor man's vacuum" and it works quite well at preventing the meat from becoming freezer burned.

By late afternoon we were on the way back to the lodge in the wheel plane with one whole and most of a second tenderloin, along with fresh eggs, vegetables, and a gallon of ice cream to share with the crew.

The Narcoleptic Visitor

As we flew the one hundred eighteen miles to the lodge, I sashayed along the route in hopes of showing Ray some more game. On the hunting menu we still had one course of black bear and moose to serve to Bob, as well a double dose of caribou. Aircraft sightings of game as we traveled just served as a tasty appetizer for the main dish, yet to come.

Things had so far gone so well, I wondered if our luck could hold out.

We saw more than twenty moose on the flight of which eight were mature bulls, but none were satisfactory, especially after taking that one with Ray. I was hoping to find an especially impressive rack for Bob, but I knew the equal of Ray's might take years … or a lifetime to locate.

As I flew over the lodge and went up creek a ways before making my down wind turn I was shocked to see orange signal smoke billowing up from a patch of willows a few hundred yards northwest of the lodge.

What the heck?

We landed and were greeted by Bob, my Dad, my sister and Max, our lab. I asked what was going on with the smoke signal, but none of them had seen it. In fact it was not visible from the lodge due to the dense willow growth.

My Dad, Pop we called him, unloaded the cub with special attention to the well insulated ice cream.

Ray, Bob and I walked over to the source of the smoke. We found a smoke flare still emitting its orange vapors. Inside the tent amidst a hastily strewn collection of Mountain House meal packages, a sleeping bag and back pack, laid a large man. His cloths were in disarray and he appeared to be upset.

When I said hello, the man sat bolt upright and glared at me as he grabbed his 45/70 single shot rifle.

"Its okay, we are friends," I assured him as he began to lift the weapon.

The fellow dropped the rifle and struggled to get up. I extended my hand and assisted him. This guy was big, weighing more than three hundred pounds. I took a step forward to avoid being pulled off my feet. Upright, the man was shaky.

"Its a good day to die," he said.

"Its never a good day to die," I corrected him. Immediately I recalled the movie "Little BIg Man" and figured this guy was some sort of semi-wacko, or a wannabe Indian.

When he had seemed to gather himself mentally I asked what he was doing there and why he had not just walked over to the lodge. We could see the top of the roof from where we stood in front of his tent.

The man told us that he had been dropped off on a river on the north slope and planned to hike to the Noatak River, about forty air miles south of the lodge. Following the meandering, braided Trail Creek, he would have to walk closer to sixty or eighty miles to get to the river. He would have to make several hazardous river crossings as well.

Several empty shell casings for his rifle were on the ground. He said he had only three rounds left. He had discharged several shots in the past two days and was hoping that he would not need those remaining to defend himself from a Grizzly.

Again I pointed to the lodge and said he should have just gone over. He said he had not seen the building, but he thought he heard a generator the night before. My Dad had started our 1500 Watt generator that evening to call my wife Mae in Kotzebue on the Single Side Band radio.

Well, this was bizarre, to say the least. I told him we would help him strike his camp and escort him to the lodge. Supper would be served soon and he could eat and stay the night with us. He told me he wanted to go to Kotzebue as soon as possible. For me, this meant a minimum of three hours flying and a full day during which I could not participate in guiding activities after flying. I was not happy about the situation, but I saw no alternative to transporting him to town the following day.

The fellow was pleasant enough in the lodge, but clearly had some odd notions about life and society. It was clear that he was extremely liberal politically. After listening to a few of his thoughts on social justice and such concepts, I noticed that everyone was recoiling from the guy's body odor

The Narcoleptic Visitor

... and liberal views. Our new guest was sitting alone on the couch farthest removed from the rest of the group. No doubt he had gone without bathing for a long time, and that compounded with his obesity resulted in nauseating odors sensed by everyone but himself.

To remedy the situation I announced that it was sauna night and went to fire up the stove. When the crew and guests were back in the house I awoke the new guy from his sonorous oblivion and suggested that we might sauna together. I did not like the idea of him being alone around fire, sharp objects or anything else that might be dangerous.

When we entered the hundred and ten degree sauna room he gasped, then attempted to climb to the highest seat. I feared he might fall onto the stove, injure himself, or break the one inch cedar slats that made the bench, so I told him to use the lowest seat. Temperatures are not so elevated at the lower level.

In the dry heat of the sauna the fellow was soon drenched in sweat, adding to his already pungent odor, but I was sure once enough poison oozed its way out, he would not be so noticeable.

During our bake time he told me that he suffered from narcolepsy. He could not overcome the urge to sleep and sometimes he was afflicted by the uncontrollable need in the midst of activities that put him at risk. He said the hike he was on was intended to be a sort of communication with his God and he hoped to beat the sleep disorder or he would die trying.

Suddenly I felt sympathy for the fellow, so cursed as he was with that awful handicap. I uttered a silent prayer of thanks that neither I nor my family suffered from the aliment and I prayed that our guest would be given relief. I felt more tolerant of the man, but still kept a close eye on him, lest he wreak some sort of unintended havok before he departed.

Bob expressed concern that losing a day of hunting was not good, but I suggested that he and Ray spend the time I was away fishing or hunting ptarmigan. I felt caught between a rock and a hard place, but taking the fellow to town was clearly a necessity.

Before the morning sunlight kissed the lodge, our surprise guest and I were in the air for Kotzebue. Due to his bulk, it was a chore loading the man in the passenger seat, but with the assistance of Pop and a reinforced milk crate as a stepping platform, we managed to stuff him inside. The clam shell door kept popping open during the ninety minute flight to town. The guy was just too big for a super cub. When we landed he asked me what he owed me and I told him that he owed exactly nothing and I wished him the best of luck and that God Bless him.

Back to the Hunt

My wife, the passenger and I had a light lunch. I gassed up the plane, then loaded some lumber and fuel oil. I always avoided making a flight that was not maxed out with things that could eventually be used. My flight back to the lodge was pleasant.

As I flew directly over the Noatak flats toward the mouth of the Kuguroruk River I noticed fresh moose tracks in the mud near a huge round lake in the middle of the tundra. The lake had a good growth of willows on the east side and I saw the outstanding white antlers of a big moose that had just shed its velvet. I had never before hunted around this lake as it did not appear to be a likely place, sitting in the bare tundra with only a few trees at its easterly margin, but this moose was a dandy that I estimated to have a spread of about sixty-five inches with great palms, lots of points and wonderful symmetry. This bull was not as exceptional as Ray's, but it was far better than most and meat packing would be a short distance. It was not a bull to pass up. This would be a dandy trophy for Bob.

Had it not been for the surprise guest at the lodge I likely never would have seen that big moose. The experience with the unexpected guest had a silver lining, it seemed.

Upon landing at the lodge I told Bob that he should get packed as we were going back to town where we would transfer to the float plane and put in a camp that evening for that big bull I had found.

Mae was surprised to see me back in town that same afternoon. She prepared a quick supper for Bob and me before we flew up to the big tundra lake.

When we reached the lake, the big bull was feeding out in the water over one hundred yards from the shore. There were no other lakes within walking distance to use for our overnight camp. Bob liked the looks of the moose, but I cautioned him that our landing may spook the animal, however it was our only option. I landed on the far side of the lake in full view of the feeding moose. As we glided toward a narrow peninsula behind

The Narcoleptic Visitor

which we could conceal the plane and tent, the bull was looking at us with water and lily fronds drooling from his mouth, then it went back to feeding.

After beaching the plane I peered over the tundra and saw the moose still feeding in the same place. Three more bulls and several cows had entered the lake for an evening snack. There was no mistaking which was the biggest bull.

We were forced to camp in uncomfortable proximity to our quarry, so absolute silence was observed. A cacophony of loon calls eerily greeted nightfall. A flight of a dozen pintail ducks landed close to the tent. I was satisfied that we were as unobtrusive as possible in that open area.

That night I was awakened twice by splashing sounds. There was no sign of beavers, so I decided the moose were likely responsible for the noises, but I slept fitfully. Before daylight I had the thermos of coffee and grocery pastries ready for Bob and I to chew on as we waited for the sun.

As the visibility improved I could see no moose in the water and the open mud flats to the east were vacant, as well. We made our way toward the willows on the far side of the lake. From a point about six hundred yards away I picked up the headlight glint of the large antlers, gathering and reflecting the sun's rays. Our big moose was standing in the thickest part of the willows, which was to our advantage. The animal was feeding, browsing on willows, and surrounded by several other moose. A slight wind was blowing from us toward the moose, so we walked south to avoid broadcasting our smell directly to the quarry. Using what cover we could we slowly approached the mob of moose. Most animals are more easily stalked from above, so we skirted the margin of the lake to come up on the ridge directly above and down wind from the thicket that held the moose.

This stalk was almost too easy. The great bull was directly below us at about ninety yards, blissfully munching on the tops of the new willow shoots.

I told Bob to let me know before he shot, but take his time and hold for the neck. Pipe in his mouth as usual, but unlit that morning, Bob held and shot true. The moose collapsed where he was standing. Before packing and lighting his pipe Bob inspected his trophy and voiced his approval.

Bob and his superb moose

As fine as the sixty-six inch rack was, Bob preferred a European style display, so I did not take the cape on this animal. We butchered it in standard fashion and had only a short distance to take the loads of meat to the lake shore. We were back in town with Bob and the first load by noon and by six o'clock we were once again airborne and headed southeast to the blueberry bogs in search of a black bear..

The fellow with narcolepsy had left two hundred dollars in cash with my wife, Mae, at the store. I was humbled by his act. I really did not expect or want any compensation for my small service.

Blueberry Bob

A thought kept creeping into my consciousness - how long can this weather remain so unblemished by adverse storms? We continued to make the best use of the ideal conditions. Bob and I flew to the same general area I had taken Ray only four days before. We saw plenty of bears, all busy slurping down as many of the sweet wild blueberries as they could.

The tent went up and without a fire we enjoyed one of the fine bottles of wine that Bob and Ray had brought from their cellars in Boston.

The natural serenade of loons, ducks and high flying geese made for an idyllic evening.

Morning found us sipping coffee poured from the thermos and swallowing store bought bear claw pastries. I never get tired of those treats.

We started walking toward the area that gave us Ray's bear. We saw more bears this day than before, and time was on our side. We glassed over a dozen bears, none of which became aware of our intrusion. Bob took great interest in some Tundra swans, whose grey colored chicks, or signets, were nearly mature enough to fly. We saw several beavers swimming across their home lakes with fresh birch branches in their mouths.

It was the end of summer and the wild critters were making ready for the vicissitudes of the coming harsh winter.

High cirrus clouds hinted at a change in weather. I mentioned that to Bob and suggested that we were surely due for some conditions less desirable than we had so far experienced.

After scrutinizing several more bears we settled on one that appeared to be noticeably larger. Upon stalking within one hundred yards I spotted

"Blueberry Bob" and his black bear boar.

a small black form near the larger bear. We were stalking a sow with a single small cub.

We broke off the pursuit and took a circuitous route toward the tent when we saw another bear that had promise. Unfortunately it was feeding in a brushy area, rather than an open berry bog. After watching it for an hour and seeing no sign of cubs, we moved in closer. I felt confident that it was a lone bear and told Bob to take it.

When the bullet struck the bear it took off like a rocket, bounding straight ahead. It went about seventy yards before taking a head over heels tumble. I was sure its action indicated it had been hit in the heart. When we came to the dark form it did not move. Its eyes were wide open in a stark, lifeless stare.

In skinning the bear I related to Bob that the Indians around Iliamna Lake had asked me to tie off the ends of the stomach of black bears to bring to them. In August and September one normally finds only blue berries in black bear stomachs and this makes for easy pickings. Bob thought that sounded like a capital idea, so I did it for him. Once I had the over stuffed stomach in hand I untied one end and squeezed out some of the contents.

The Narcoleptic Visitor

It was pure blue berries, most of which had been chewed. Bob slurped up a handful and pronounced it delicious. From then on, he enjoyed being referred to as "Blueberry Bob."

With only two caribou left to locate and not enough time to get to town and on to the lodge, we spent that night in the tent after I had removed the head and paws from the skin, and flew to town the next day.

Our old chest freezer was filling rapidly with the trophies taken by our two guests. I was able to put some of the meat and hides in the freezer of a local fish buyer. In busy times like these, I normally fleshed and lightly salted the capes and hides before freezing them to send to taxidermists. I folded and fitted Bob's bear skin inside and we were off to Trail Creek. Ray's moose meat, prepared and frozen, would suffice for our winter needs, so the nearly eight hundred pounds of meat from Bob's bull was shared with family and friends. In a fall with good hunting we normally had well over a ton of prime meat to give away.

Bonus Wolf

We landed before eight in the evening and were pleased to learn that Ray had shot a large black male wolf from the lodge window that morning. Pop had seen the wolf sitting on a small knoll about one hundred fifty yards from the building and Ray rested his rifle on the window sill and smoked the lobo. My Dad had skinned it and the hide was hanging from our meat pole. We seldom sighted wolves during fall hunts until the early 1990s. Apparently by then the increased protection of wolves and restrictions on their taking (no more shotgunning from an airplane and no state bounty

This is a large mature male wolf.

Ray and Pop with the window wolf.

after 1976) had led to a huge increase in the population of the wild canines throughout Alaska. Since the 1990s we frequently see wolves around the lodge - sometimes on a daily basis, and sightings when flying to and from Kotzebue have become common.

Barren Ground Caribou

For the past week, more and more caribou were filtering through the valley of Trail Creek on their annual migration to their wintering grounds in the south. Pop and Pat had reported some large bulls bringing up the tail ends of bands made up mostly of cows and calves. It usually begins that way.

The next morning we located groups of caribou to the northwest and southwest of the lodge, but none included any trophy bulls. We spent the day pleasurably looking over the dozens which soon numbered in the hundreds of the tundra deer as they moved down the valley, but still we found no bulls worthy of pursuit.

It was still legal to hunt caribou the same day airborne in 1983, so I decided to take one of the hunters in the plane the next day to get a feel for what might be coming our way from the North Slope. It was Ray's turn. Bob said he would be content to remain at the lodge, enjoying his pipe and blueberries.

We steered through the summit peaks of the western Brooks Range and down the Utukok River to a bank near a stream called Driftwood and landed. Caribou seemed to be growing from the tundra. Thousands of the animals were loitering over the hills as far as our eyes could see.

Ray picked out a rack that he liked. It was of the type I call a "spider head" as it had long points, a wide spread, but very little sign of palmation. We waded across the Utukok River and hiked toward the selected animal.

Arctic ground squirrels squealed their protests at our trespass of their home areas. Arctic terns swooped close to our heads when we passed too close to their nests along the stream. A snowy owl flew by, looking us over, as we began to climb the rolling hill toward the intended trophy.

Lone caribou can often be lured to a hunter by simply raising one's rifle butt high as he bends over and moves slowly, emulating a feeding caribou bull, but in this large mob, we had no success in our efforts to bring the target bull closer to us. A cow near our bull startled and charged through the knee and ankle wrenching tundra with ease, taking our bull with her. We stopped and waited until the cow went back to feeding along a small creek, then we dropped below a rise in the terrane and humped along to close the distance between us and the bull. We spent over two hours stalking until finally we were within two hundred yards of the bull.

Ray was confident he could make the shot, so I told him to settle into the tundra for a rest, take his time, and fire when ready. Ray's confidence was matched by his competence and the bull dropped in its tracks. We butchered the bull similar to the way we did moose, but with far less strain and weight to pack. Then we headed back to the airplane with me carrying the meat and Ray taking the rack. He decided on a European mount for this animal. We had a pack of just a little over two miles directly to the airplane.

Ray and his "spider head" caribou.

Our stalk had taken longer than anticipated, so we hurried to tie the rack on the wing struts, load the meat on a blue tarp behind Ray's seat, piled the tent, sleeping bags and camping gear on top of the meat and took off for home. As we flew through the head of Trail Creek the hills were dotted with caribou heading south toward the lodge.

Unlike many Alaskan's, I prefer caribou meat to that of moose, but I also believe that the caribou in the far northwest have better tasting flesh than those of more southerly parts of the state. The next morning we enjoyed caribou steaks and eggs and our guests concurred regarding the flavor of *Rangifer tarandus*.

Well rested, Bob wanted to have a go at caribou the next morning, but when we had light enough to see, we were surrounded by hundreds of caribou in all quadrants from the lodge. We could not hope to do better than take advantage of the situation right in our own back yard. This is often the case.

Just after ten o'clock in the morning, a band of approximately six hundred caribou came by on the east side of the lodge. Bringing up the

ALASKA NORTHWEST ARCTIC HUNTS

Cabin in center of photo. When they're in the yard, there's no need to look elsewhere.

Bob's caribou from the swamp next to the lodge.

rear were several huge bulls. We needed only to walk to the outhouse, conceal ourselves in the willows and select the one Bob wanted. Under such stress free conditions, Bob dropped a good bull and we all appreciated the short distance we had to move the meat to hang on the rack.

Bob decided on a shoulder mount for his bull, so I cut the carcass in half, upended the front half to drain before I caped it. I carried the hind half to the meat rack and hung it.

Somehow, the three weeks time had slipped by much too rapidly for us all. Both men decided against taking another caribou, though they legally could have taken up to five each. Ptarmigan hunting and fishing for grayling

Ray and Bob with their two outstanding Moose

Ray and Bob with their northwest Arctic Alaskan collection.

and Arctic char kept them entertained for the two days remaining before they had to head back to Boston. Their taxidermist said they had each collected as fine a bag of four big game species as he had ever seen. And Ray had taken the large male wolf.

Ray telephoned to tell me that the taxidermist was able to save the velvet on his moose rack. That seventy-six and a half inch set of antlers won him a beautiful walnut plaque for second place moose the 1983/84 Safari Club International/ Alaska Professional Hunters Club all Alaska Big Game Trophy Competition.

In January of 1985 Bob, Ray, my Dad, and I all attended the Safari Club International's annual convention in Las Vegas. Rays huge moose was displayed in the main show room.

I was surprised to see Ray's "spider head" caribou on display.

Neither Dad nor I could buy a single cocktail as Ray had paid the hotel for all our expenses.

All of their trophies were fine examples of their species, as were our guests, Bob and Ray.

Some Events of 1984

In 1984 I had a family from Florida at the lodge. The man, I will call Geoff, came to hunt, bringing his wife, Viki, and their ten year old son, Junior, along for some fishing and other Alaskan experiences. Geoff was especially interested in taking a grizzly and a Dall ram.

When I met the family at the airport, Geoff was a bit under the weather from imbibing too much fire water during his long flight from Florida. His wife suggested that I take him to the hospital and keep him from drinking during his stay with us. I told her I would take him to the hospital, but I was contracted to be his guide, not his AA counselor or jailer. If his drinking was such that I felt he endangered himself or others, I would terminate the contract.

Geoff stayed in town with me while his wife and son boarded the charter plane to the lodge with my son Martin. The doctor told him to sober up.

After a good night's sleep we flew out in my super cub on floats and after only an hour of uneventful travel we flew over a mature bull moose. A lake of adequate size sat a convenient half mile from the moose, so I landed. The perimeter of this lake, like many in the area, contained a mat of floating moss-like vegetation which was spongy to walk on and occasionally parted to thrust a person into deep water. I cautioned Geoff to remain at least three feet behind me as I carried a rope to secure the airplane and gingerly trod my way toward the shore. Geoff followed my directions but half way to firm footing he broke through the floating mat and filled his hip boots with moss and water. He had the presence of mind to not holler. I tossed him the loose end of rope and pulled him toward me. His rifle action was submerged, so I immediately disassembled the bolt of his Winchester Model 70 and thoroughly dried, then tested it. Geoff turned his hip boots inside out and set them on a rack we made out of sticks. There was no wind, so a small fire would soon help drive the moisture from his boots.

We set up the tent and tucked in. At first light we proceeded toward the area that held the bull and found him feeding in the birch and willow brush, accompanied by three other bulls. The stalk was quick and easy. Geoff soon had a very respectable moose on the ground with minimal distance for me to pack the meat.

Geoff was immediately energized when he saw the size of the antlers. He happily

Geoff's beautiful moose rack.

helped me pack the meat to the lake and we flew back to town that same evening with the trophy, the camp and part of the meat. After some pan fried moose back strap and a baked potato, we each enjoyed a hearty libation from one of Geoff's several bottles. He enjoyed the good stuff.

The following morning I set off to retrieve the rest of the meat, leaving Geoff in his sleeping bag at my town shack.

As I flew the load of meat to Kotzebue I passed over a large band of caribou which held some respectable bulls.

After placing the meat in the freezer, we loaded up in the float plane again and headed back to the caribou. It was legal in those days to land and shoot caribou the same day one was airborne, so we landed a mile from the herd and headed for the mob of tundra deer.

We had plenty of cover in scrub willow and birch and were within easy shooting range of the animals in thirty minutes. We could evaluate about a hundred and fifty animals from our position, so we held until I could pick out a worthy bull. It was still August, so most of the animals carried velvet on their antlers. Geoff didn't mind that.

Using my forked walking stick to steady his aim, Geoff shot a good bull to add to his trophy collection. We set up the tent and spent a second night in the wilds of northwest Alaska. We enjoyed a shot of Geoff's whiskey and a rack of fresh grilled caribou ribs before crawling into our sacks

Some Events of 1984

Another trophy so quickly made the hunting seem too easy.

When we returned to the lodge, the sunny, windless day indicated it was time for some family fishing, so Martin and I escorted the family down Trail Creek that afternoon. Geoff and I each had our rifle in case of need. We found the Arctic Char and Grayling were eager to take any lure we presented. Again, things just seemed to be coming too easily. The Florida folks did not appreciate how extraordinarily simple their trophy quest was going. Geoff mentioned that hunting and fishing here was better than he had encountered anywhere in Africa on his several trips to the dark continent.

A nice family catch of Arctic Char - taken less than a mile from the lodge and 155 miles north of the Arctic Circle

A few days into the family's booking I flew to Kotzebue to meet my friend, Peter Johnstone, a Professional Hunter from Rhodesia with whom I had traded a hunt in 1982. Upon landing at the lodge strip with Peter, Geoff and Junior ran up breathlessly, advising me that they had just seen a large blond grizzly, a few hundred meters off the end of the runway.

As I was on final approach to touch down, I'd noticed a large, light colored porcupine (*Erethizon dorsatum*) feeding on dwarf birch brush in the area they described.

Many times in the past I had mistaken a porcupine for a lumbering grizzly bear, so I confidently assumed that Geoff had been similarly fooled. The fat-laden quill pigs all seem to walk with a rolling motion, not unlike that of a ponderous old bear.

Geoff and Junior were getting more excited by the minute, retelling their story, obviously expecting me to react quickly, rush down there and see to it that Geoff anchored that big grizz.

We secured the airplane and leisurely carried Peter's gear and the fresh groceries to the lodge. We did not hurry, as Geoff continued to talk about that big bear he'd just seen. Junior was nearly jumping up and down.

We sat down in the great room of the lodge and I poured a gin and tonic for Peter and one for myself, offering one to Geoff, whose anxiety was mounting.

After a sip, I suggested to Geoff that he and Junior just go on down and shoot that thing.

Everyone present seemed taken aback by my nonchalant comment. I said, "Well, I guess you better get at it, eh?" "And oh, Junior, better pack my .22 rifle along, just in case."

I added that if he wanted a rug to be made from the hide, he could skin it right there after he was right sure it was dead.

Geoff muttered an "Uh huh." and departed, shaking his head in disbelief.

When the pair was out of earshot, Peter asked me, "Jake, you're sending your clients down there on their own after dangerous game .. and with only one big bore rifle ?"

I had another sip of my cocktail and said, "Sure, they'll be fine, you'll see."

Peter muttered that an African Professional Hunter would risk revocation of his license by committing such an irresponsible action.

Viki seemed apprehensive, but I assured her that it would turn out well. However, my comment did not seem to assuage her motherly and wifely concerns.

Before our glasses were drained, several shots were heard. Viki, Peter, and the cook were immediately plastered at the window - their noses actually left oily marks on it . There they remained, transfixed for twenty minutes after which time they reported that Geoff and Junior were coming back and neither was limping. Viki expressed her relief that her only child was not harmed. Kathy, the cook shot me a quizzical glance. I winked at her.

When the stalwart hunters joined us they sat down and said nothing. Viki asked what happened. Peter and Kathy were lazer focused, waiting for the response.

Geoff reported, "Well, he was a big un, all right," but he wasn't sure how Viki would like for it to be skinned, so he left that for Jake to do. That was a nice touch on his part, which I appreciated.

We all six waked down to see the big bear, which, mysteriously, had transformed itself into a blonde porcupine! Geoff and Junior erupted in raucous laughter. They'd played their unscripted parts well and we all enjoyed a wonderful beginning of the two weeks that we would spend together. Humor is truly invaluable.

Guests universally seem incredulous at the presence of porcupines so far above the coniferous tree line. I felt the same way initially, but we see a quillrat about once per year. They do not hibernate, so how, with nothing even close to fur, they survive sixty degrees below zero and colder? Its a mystery.

During the years I had a labrador dog at the lodge, I dispatched most of the porcupines I found in the area, as dogs find meddling with the quill pigs irresistible and porcupine quills in the face and tongue of any dog are excruciating at best, and sometimes fatal. I once found a recently deceased adult wolf with a face and mouth full of quills.

Earlier, before Johnstone arrived, my son, Martin had been assisting me. As we prepared to take Geoff up into West Bowl for a ram, Martin was using a large pack of mine. The panel which separated the top compartment from the lower one had torn out and in an attempt to keep the load from settling to the bottom, Martin blew up a heavy plastic bag and stuffed it into the lower part of the large compartment. Geoff asked why he was doing that. Without hesitation, Martin pointed to the peaks and told him that we were ascending to altitudes where the air was thinner, so he thought it a good idea to take a little extra air along. I was right proud of Martin and his explanation. It seemed his long and close association with me and my spontaneous B.S. was paying off.

Geoff slowly nodded as he said "Uh huh."

In spite of the extra air, we were unsuccessful in our attempt to provide Geoff an opportunity to secure a ram that day.

One evening after supper, Geoff had consumed a bit too much rum again and was lying in his bunk when I glassed two full curl rams across the creek. They descended through a large shale slide to an uncharacteristically low level. I went below to waken Geoff and told him this was a great opportunity for him to collect his ram.

He got booted up quickly and we headed for the rams, with my trusty labrador dog, Max, at my heel.

We waded across Trail Creek and worked our way up through the cottonwoods and willows to a point about 150 yards below the rams. Geoff, using a forked stick to steady his aim, held for just behind the shoulder and squeezed . The bullet struck the ram in the spine and it tumbled down through the loose rock rolling over and over, before stopping in the pucker brush a few yards from us.

Geoff with his slipped horn ram.

But, when we got to the ram, we saw that the right horn had slipped off, leaving only a bloody boss. Geoff was a normally calm fellow, but he did a little cursing at the sight of his damaged trophy. I told him not to worry as I searched the shale and bushes for the horn. Darn! I couldn't locate that horn! I caped the ram and we got meat, cape and head back to camp before dark. I was surprised at not fining the missing horn.

However I saw a similar situation in the Wrangle Mountains. The guide I was assisting, the hunter and I were unable to locate the missing horn. A taxidermist could fabricate one, of course, but it was still a great disappointment for all three of us. Additionally the big ram could not be entered in the record book. I did not mention this to Geoff. Plus, this time we had Max's nose on our side.

Geoff had a few more drinks and began to voice his worries about that horn. I told him that the dog and I would return in the morning and we would surely do our best to find it.

Next morning, after breakfast, all six humans and my one Labrador Retriever were on that shale slide. In a few minutes, Max had located it. He came back to us with the bloody, but still perfect horn in his mouth, wagging his tail. He knew he was the hero of the moment!

Sheep horns are tough and I've never seen one get broken in a fall, but they do occasionally slip completely off, as happened in this case and only one other in my experiences with over a hundred and twenty ram kills.

Geoff had taken a good bull moose and a fine caribou, but he had missed a nice Grizzly near the lodge as his son watched. He was embarrassed by his poor shooting and I felt remorse for both him and his son.

Near the end of his booking Geoff and I were about three and a half miles south of the lodge when we found another good lone Grizzly. It was across a small branch of the creek from us, feeding on tubers called massu, or Eskimo potato. We stalked to within forty yards. I had my Super 8 mm movie camera running as Geoff shot. The impact rocked the bruin and I told Geoff to keep shooting, which he did, but apparently he missed the next two shots. I had plenty of time to shoot also, but I seldom do, unless the animal seems about to escape. I soon wished I had shot that bear, because it got into heavy brush and we lost it. Plenty of blood indicated a good hit, but I felt like it was liver shot, rather than hit in the lungs.

On my mind, motivating me, was the fact that Geoff had missed an easy shot on a bear and his son had seen it. I wanted the boy to see the film showing his Dad making the kill without assistance, for the boy's sake, primarily. That should not have been my primary focus.

For the next two days, Max and I searched for that bear, but we were unsuccessful. Ravens led me to the carcass five days later in the dense pucker brush near where it had been shot. It had died not more than 200 yards from where it had been shot, but had lingered alive for a considerable time, possibly a couple miserable days after its encounter with us.

That is the only big game animal other than two wolves and one Sitka blacktail deer, that I have lost in more than fifty years of hunting and guiding in Alaska. The hide was not salvageable, but would have squared about seven and a half feet. It was an old boar with a previously fractured mandible, most likely from being kicked by a moose. The animal was not in robust condition.

It was my fault. I should have shot when I had the chance.

Overall, our Florida guests were pleased with their time in the Arctic and invited me to their home. In 1986 I spent a few days fishing for large mouth Bass and enjoyed some wonderful meals with them. Geoff's three superb Alaska big game trophies occupied preferred positions in his large game room.

Geoff passed away eight years later and his wife called to tell me the bad news. She said the family had reminisced about their time in Alaska hunting with me many times.

An African Professional Hunter Guest

In September, 1984, after our Florida guests departed, Peter Johnstone, a Professional Hunter from Southern Rhodesia (now called Zimbabwe), and I were joined by a state moose biologist, Bill Gasaway, who had known Peter for many years and hunted with him in Rhodesia on one occasion. It was Gasaway who introduced me to Peter and that led to our swapping hunts in 1982. The swap was as good as one can be - for both parties.

Bill loved to hunt and especially enjoyed calling moose. He usually brought his own super cub and was always great company. Bill had helped me as an Assistant Guide and had also enjoyed the use of the lodge in my absences or before the guest hunters arrived on a couple of previous occasions. Bill Gasaway was a most trusted and valued friend.

With Bill practicing his calling as I took mental notes and filmed, Peter took a huge bull moose just a half mile north of the lodge. It placed #3 in the Safari Club International/ Alaska Professional Hunters Association's first Big Three Competition which included the hunting seasons of 1983 and 1984. I had seen that bull off and on for more than two months. One evening it walked up the runway, but we spotted it too late and did not get an opportunity for Peter to shoot. I reckoned that chances were good that it would enter a large willow thicket about a half mile up creek that held several cows. Hopefully the bull would find them and they all would still be there in the morning.

Before daylight, Peter, Bill and I were on a tall cut bank on the west side of Trail Creek, across the stream from the big willow patch, when Bill began calling. A cow answered us and soon thereafter we heard the thrashing noises of a bull attacking willows. After less than half an hour of Bill's patient coaxing, the bull stepped out of the thicket and onto an open gravel

I'm over six feet tall, but Peter Johnstone, right, is one BIG hunter!

bar, where Peter dropped him with a chest shot. It was a magnificent trophy moose, shown above.

In previous discussions Peter had assured us that the Livingstone's Eland in his Rhodesian hunting concession were larger than Alaskan moose. When he looked over that draft horse-sized moose, he stepped back, shook his head in wonder, and agreed that Alaskan Moose are larger than Livingstone's Eland. When I took a bull Eland in Rhodesia with him in 1982, he assured me, over my protests, that Eland are much larger than any moose, but he'd never seen a moose in the flesh until the day he shot this one.

For ten days we had been watching a band of five rams on Middle Mountain, just east of the lodge. We used my large fifteen to sixty power tripod mounted spotting scope right from the great room of the lodge to evaluate, scrutinize, and deliberate on those rams. Two of the five were very good trophies, but we held off, waiting for something even better. Bill Gasaway was a keen trophy hunter, but he had not yet adjusted his personal standards for those of a hunter who did not live in Alaska and may not have the time or opportunities that come with residency. As Peter's time to leave approached, he and I climbed up and easily collected one of the two largest of those fine rams.

An African Professional Hunter Guest

Peter, his ram and me, with the lodge in the valley below.

In 1984 it was legal to hunt caribou the same day airborne and, one day as we were flying down to the Kuguroruk River to catch some fresh, fat, sea-run Arctic Char which are so much more tasty than those we catch near the lodge after their hundred plus mile upstream trip without feeding, we came upon several hundred caribou crossing Trail Creek just above it's confluence with the Kuguroruk. I saw several outstanding bulls in the bunch, but they were not reasonably accessible, so we landed and began to fish. The char were stacked up like cordwood in a big eddy near the mouth of Trail Creek. We soon had one for our dinner, plus an extra one to bake and use for sandwich spread the next day. As I did the pre-flight check and prepared the cub for departure, the same band of caribou came down the side of the valley toward us. This was an unanticipated gift!

We retrieved our rifles from the airplane and hustled to a line of willows close to the tail of the aircraft. A short wait was all it took for the big bull to show and Peter soon had it on the ground with a fine neck shot. It was one of the most beautiful, long-tined and symmetrical caribou that I have ever seen. Dumb luck had struck again, and this time, it was on our side.

That evening as we were flying back to the lodge I saw a huge Grizzly on a moose kill amidst some cottonwood trees and willow brush on Popple Creek, about five miles downstream from the lodge. Three big bull moose had been

Peter Johnstone with his superb Barren Ground Caribou

resting there when we flew by to go fishing. Now one of the bulls had been killed by what appeared to be the largest Grizzly that I had ever seen.

Darkness was soon to be upon us, so we baked a char and checked our rifles for the next day's hunt. We could walk the distance, but one of Peter's ankles was bothering and causing him to limp, so I decided to land the next afternoon on a nearby bar - about a half mile from the bear and set up a tent, planning to stalk the bear the following morning.

At six hundred feet above ground level we flew over the kill site to see the massive grizzly lying on top of a huge pile of debris he had raked over the carcass of the moose. The bear seemed to be embracing his fresh food cache with both his arms.

We set up the tent and did without a fire. We enjoyed a cold meal and a snort of whiskey, talking only in whispers, though we were well away from the bruin.

Dawn brought us a clear sky. The wind was light, but steady out of the north. I had fixed in my mind the precise spot where the moose kill was located and we began to cautiously, silently, ease our way closer. I had been in that very location several times over the past several years and was sure of the route.

Peter had asked me in a low whisper how many bear kills I had participated in. I hold him that it was a few less than two hundred. He said that no African guide took even one hundred lions without being mauled at least once. I emphasized that he should not discount the dangerous nature of bears and that killing most Grizzlies required more than one shot. I also mentioned that being mauled by a bear is not part of the normal history of most Alaskan guides. Those that do get mauled by a bear, usually get dead, too. I sensed that he figured bears were not as potentially dangerous as African lions, so I stressed to him that Grizzlies are truly dangerous game. In fact, all bears can be extremely dangerous.

I placed a 300 Winchester Magnum round in the chamber of my Model 70, added a round to the magazine and put the rifle on safe. Peter shoved an ought-six in his tube and engaged his safety, as well. Our magazines were full.

As we cautiously neared the spot, carefully displacing willow branches with my arms and watching where I placed my foot for each step, I touched

Peter's arm, indicating that he should be alert. I pointed and mouthed the words to him that a rounded brown spot in front of us was the bears left ear and he was looking our way. We were less than thirty-five yards from the beast. Only underbrush separated us from the nearly half ton mound of *Ursus horribilis*.

At that moment, hearing or sensing something, the bear raised its head and looked right at us. Peter fired. His bullet struck the bear just below the jaw. It dropped straight away as if a rug had been jerked out from its feet. It was on its belly and completely motionless.

Before I could restrain him, Peter shot it again in the top of the head. That second shot was an unfortunate waste, because the first had broken the neck and the head shot fractured the skull, preventing it from being entered into the Boone and Crockett Club Record Book. That skull measured over twenty-five inches and the bear was the largest in body of any inland Grizzly that I had ever seen. We measured the hide, holding the tape tight. It squared eight feet, ten inches, making it the largest interior Grizzly that I have ever measured. It looked like a coastal brown bear.

So, Peter Johnstone shot the largest Grizzly and Caribou that I had seen, as well as a dandy Dall Ram and an award winning Moose.

Our trade hunts had been absolutely wonderful for both of us. We each had enjoyed two of the best mixed bag hunts of our lifetimes. Most trade hunts do not end up anything close to that.

I wanted to take Peter in my float plane for a black bear, but his travel schedule would not allow the two or three day delay. That was a pity, with out luck running so strong, who knows what we may have found.

For several years thereafter Peter and I shared a booth at some hunting trade shows, calling our association, the Afralaska Exchange.

An African Professional Hunter Guest

Peter Johnstone and his 8'10" Grizzly.

Peter Johnstone and his four outstanding trophies.

Grizzlies, Raven, And The Snow Snake

Ravens (*Corvus corax*) are common throughout Alaska and are one of my favorite birds. They do an efficient sanitation job, quickly consuming gut piles left by hunters as well as carcasses of animals that have died of natural causes or road kill. They peck up whatever they can from predator kills. Their presence often leads hunters to kill sites that may be simultaneously attracting other predators, such as bears, wolves and wolverines, which may be of interest to the human hunters. Many times I have observed a single raven flying right over a wolf or bear, dogging the larger predator from above. I've also seen traveling bears alter their course to check out ravens that the bruin heard or saw near the ground in their vicinity. It appears that the bears are in expectation of sharing, or stealing, a meal already attended by ravens.

These intelligent avians are often seen playing in updrafts and thermals, putting on impressive air shows. I may be anthropomorphizing, but they appear to be possessed of an extraordinary intelligence, and at times, a sense of humor.

So, the two-legged hunter is well advised to play attention to ravens, as their presence may signal other live animals nearby, as well as dead ones. Once a hunter makes a kill, the arrival of ravens may bring in an unwelcome bear, which is all too common throughout Alaska and especially so on Kodiak Island.

Following the departure of a Professional Hunter from Rhodesia, Peter Johnstone, who had taken the largest inland Grizzly I have ever seen, at eight feet, ten inches squared, I welcomed a German physician named Klaus, one of my frequent guest hunters and good friend Bruce Moe, who brought a lady hunter, named Kara.

Bruce had killed a huge bear with me in 1978. That Grizzly placed in the top 50 of the Boone and Crockett Club record book. That was prior to the Grizzly permits being issued by drawing in northwest Alaska which began in 1980. Bruce applied and was drawn for a permit in 1984 and told me that he would be satisfied with a smaller bear, but he'd prefer a blond … as gentlemen are reported to do.

I had to go to Kotzebue to get a German hunter, so Bruce, Kara and my cook, Kathy, (after the death of my first wife, Mae, I had several different cooks for the fall seasons), remained at the lodge while I went to town to fetch Klaus.

As we returned to the lodge I flew over the site where Peter Johnstone had taken his giant Grizzly and found another huge bear, well over eight feet squared, feeding on the carcass of the first bear, as well as the remains of the moose.

I turned to Klaus and said, "My friend, there is you bear."

The cottonwood trees and willow brush were dense at the kill site and, as it had been with Johnstone's big bear, the shooting would likely be tense and at very close quarters.

We made two slow passes over the spot and Klaus told me, "No, Jake, I come for the tundra grizzly, not the forest bear." He did not like the thought of approaching a big grizzly on a kill at dangerously close range with such restricted visibility in heavy brush which could deflect the bullet. This fellow was using good sense, but I would have gone for it … and did so with our other guest, Bruce Moe.

At the lodge over a glass of wine I related to all what we'd found. I estimated that bear feeding on the gut piles would square well over eight feet, but it was a dark brown, far from a blond color. Bruce said he would be happy to try for that one.

The next morning we spotted an accommodating, but smaller grizzly feeding on berries across the river from the lodge. This was what Kaus had in mind, he told me. Shortly after seeing the bear, Klaus shot it on the open tundra near the lodge.

Late the next afternoon Bruce and I loaded up and flew to the moose and bear kill site. The bear was still lying on one of the piles that covered the two large carcasses. This bruin appeared to be embracing his stash of

Max and me with Klaus' grizzly.

food. He seemed to ignore the aircraft as we flew by at six hundred feet above ground level.

This time I found an adequate landing site a bit further upstream, which seemed a good idea. We tucked in and slept fitfully as snow began to fall. It was 30 degrees cooler than when Johnstone and I had camped nearby just seven days or so before.

A heavy frost formed over everything that night and the morning light was muted by ground fog. We rose and booted up, but lingered over our cups of thermos bottle coffee and sweet rolls as we waited for the fog to lift.

Shortly before noon we began walking to the spot. When we arrived, we gingerly edged up on the kill site, with utmost care, lest we spook the bear. When we had the site fully in view, to my surprise, no bear was to be seen. The only sign of life was a raven hopping about, digging at the top of the pile. The wind was calm.

We waited, expecting the bear to show itself and perhaps rush in to scare off the scavenging bird. We were alert, thinking about the bear coming up from behind us.

More than an hour passed with the raven squawking and tearing at the vegetation which covered the carcasses. The racket should have drawn the big bear if it was lying close by, I figured.

I decided to inspect the pile of brush more closely, thinking that I should be able to pick up fresh tracks in the new fallen snow. As I cast about, looking for sign, Bruce whispered to me that the raven was injured and he was going to catch it. I told him to forget the bird. Fooling with that danged thing could cost us the bear - or worse.

Dark colored bear diarrhea was all over the place. It typically takes a big bear about eight days to consume an adult moose carcass. The voracious bruins gorge themselves faster than their digestive system can efficiently handle the intake of high calorie fat and protein, resulting in runny stools. Most of the moose was still left after the first bear was killed and about a week had passed since then. I believed the second bear had only been on the site for two or three days, so I didn't want to rush things, as if we didn't get the bear that day, he would most likely keep coming back until we got an opportunity at this second big bear, or all the meat was consumed. If we didn't run him off, we had an excellent chance of collecting his hide. Patience was called for.

When I determined that I had located the most recent of the bear tracks, I motioned for Bruce to come and we began following the trail. The further we went, the more confident I was that we were on the right track. But I was puzzled as to why the huge bear was traveling so far from his pile of meat. I doubted we had spooked him.

The ground fog was lifting, but localized areas of dense fog gave our quiet pursuit an eerie, foreboding essence.

As we rounded one particularly dense clump of willows I looked ahead and glimpsed something large and brown. I gasped and Bruce, a few steps behind me, let out a spontaneous, desperate sounding gasp, as well. On a close quarters stalk like this, I always carried a live round in the chamber over a full magazine, giving me four shots, if necessary. Reflexively bringing my rifle up, I saw a huge cow moose, browsing contentedly. I wondered how it could be that the moose was so relaxed if the bear had recently passed by? So many unusual things that day! But we continued following the fresh appearing tracks.

Well, at least I knew our tracking was quiet enough to not have spooked the moose.

After a half hour we came to small clearing. A big, dark colored bruin appeared at the far side, about 70 yards from us and was casually walking away. I told Bruce to shoot. He did and I heard the bullet hit the bear. Bruce got one more shot off before the beast disappeared from view. I ran forward and climbed up on a small esker of about twelve feet in height with Bruce right behind me.

We could see where the bear was when Bruce shot and splotches of blood were evident in the snow where the tracks led into thicker undergrowth. I figured the copious splotches of blood indicated a good lung hit. I decided we should wait on that elevated spot for a few minutes, so I lit a cigar and enjoyed the pause. We could approximately parallel the route of the bear by walking along the esker, staying above the level the bear was on, so we slowly proceeded, catching glimpses of more blood on the new snow as we eased along the way. Our elevation gave us a better view of the bush cluttered river bottom.

Then I saw the tracks turn sharply to the left and at the base of a thick bush less than ten yards back along his route was the bear, lying and watching his back trail. He had turned back on his trail and was set up to attack whatever had been chasing and wounding him.

Using hand signals to avoid noise, I pointed the bear's position to Bruce. He located the animal and shot again.

Immediately the bear rushed toward his just-laid trail. He would have been on top of us if we had followed his tracks.

Bruce shot again. In all, he shot that bear seven times with his .270. The big bear laid dead on the snow in clear sight of us. It was lying in it's own trail that it had been watching so closely.

I recovered my half smoked cigar from where it had fallen from my mouth and accompanied Bruce to his bear.

We discussed how that beast had been watching his back trail and was so well positioned to nail anything that was following. With only a few feet between the wounded Grizz and its trail, it would have overpowered any man, likely before he could get a shot off, and could have killed a hunter in seconds.

Bruce and his dandy interior Grizzly.

We worked together skinning the trophy, leaving the head and paws in the skin, to be removed at the lodge.

As we were packing out, Bruce wanted to check on the injured raven. As we had taken a life, he argued, perhaps the German doctor, Klaus, could help this bird, thereby saving a life. This time, I relented on the issue. The bird was still pecking and scratching at the meat pile, but hopped away when Bruce approached it. After both Bruce and the bird had experienced a few slips and falls in the snow, Bruce caught it.

Then the raven really began making a racket. I cautioned Bruce to be careful to protect his eyes from the beak.

When we loaded the cub, I placed the live raven in a gunny sack, twisted the top and tied it. Somehow, on the flight back, the bird got loose and was caw, caw, cawing as it thrashed about in the cabin. It spewed forth a line of poop, some of which hit the back of my head and part of that squirted fecal deposit festooned the instrument panel. I hollered at Bruce to grab that infernal flightless pest and hang onto it, or throw it out the window. He did restrain it, in spite of getting pecked and pooped on as the panicked bird struggled for freedom.

Grizzlies, Raven, And The Snow Snake

Bruce and his trophy raven. Bear hide on the ground at his right.

Once safely landed and in the tie downs at Trail Creek, I put the raven back in the sack and tied it securely. The bird went quiet as we took our gear to the lodge. I figured, and hoped, the avian critter was just plain pooped out.

Kathy, my cook, poured wine for everyone and after a hearty toast, I brought the sack upstairs and placed it on the living room rug. When the sack moved, the women noticed it, stepped well back, and with eyebrows raised, asked what was inside.

As I winked at Bruce I explained that we might have found a rare snow snake.

Kara shrieked and Kathy retreated toward the stove. The sack moved again. My Labrador, Max, who had been sniffing us, and had been preoccupied with taking in the bear smell, took sudden interest in the sack. The sack moved again, the dog jumped back and the ladies hollered and commanded me to get the infernal serpent out of the house.

By then, Bruce was laughing as I showed them all the "snow snake."

The ladies fell in love with the injured bird. Klaus diagnosed a dislocated wing joint and used two tongue depressors to cobble together a splint, during which procedure the bird defecated on his lap so we decided to tether our feathered patient and leave it in the small guide shack where it would be safe from foxes, weasels and lynx … and we would be safe from its defecatory assaults.

When we checked the shack the next day, the bird had pooped all over everything it could reach on the tether. How any critter could have such a reservoir of offal, I don't know. We fed it scraps of meat and fat which it gobbled up, but the bird died after another day or so. The stress of our company probably did the bird in.

The caribou decided to come south en masse the following day. We had superb selectivity of trophies as hundreds, and on some days thousands of the tundra deer, traipsed by the lodge. Kara took the first bull, about two miles up creek from the lodge. This was her first big game kill, and it was a dandy.

Sometimes having so many mature animals to choose from makes it difficult to finally settle on which one to shoot. In large masses, often the best heads walk free if they offer no opportunity to shoot that is clear of others in their group.

Sadly, we were unable to maneuver to get an opportunity for two outstanding bulls that kept to the middle of one rapidly moving band as they hurried south.

The lady's first big game kill.

Bruce with his first big bull.

But Bruce is a patient hunter and having taken a lot of game animals, he understood the importance of waiting for the right moment. On the next to the last day of his booking, he dumped a fine, old bull.

Bruce and Kara had each taken some impressive caribou and Bruce decided that he would use his to have a diorama done, using the raven and the bear over the caribou, so he wrapped the deceased bird carefully in one of his spare T-shirts to transport to a taxidermist.

Large bands of southward migrating caribou just kept

Bruce with his second Caribou bull of the trip.

coming down Trail Creek, so after mulling over the thought of using his bull in the diorama, Bruce decided he had best purchase another non resident tag and take one more big bull for a shoulder mount.

Adding another big bull to the stack of meat, antlers and hides to be taken to Kotzebue and eventually on to Anchorage and then points south was not a difficult chore with so much animal traffic on Trail Creek, and that same evening, Bruce scored again.

The meat was packaged in Kotzebue, with that destined for Bruce's larder shipped directly to Seattle. His hides and the raven were to be left with a taxidermist in Anchorage for tanning, then mounting. When the taxidermist saw the raven he told Bruce to get rid of it, as it was a federally protected bird and could land us all in a lot of hot water, no matter what the circumstances of its demise had been.

So that beautiful raven wound up in the nearest dumpster.

And, as for ravens, I say "Nevermore."

Two Brothers From West Germany

In 1987 we had two West German brothers who came to hunt. It was their first trip to Alaska. They had been referred by previous guests of ours, as was the case with many of our first time visitors.

Game sightings and activity had been slower than usual at Trail Creek, so after meeting their jet in Kotzebue, I flew Chris to the lodge, leaving him with my two Assistant Guides, Tom and Joe, and my labrador, Max. I returned to take Walter in the float plane to an area that had been producing big bull moose for us. After a few days we returned to Kotzebue with a dandy bull. We spent the night in my sod shack, dining on moose tenderloin filet mignon, baked potatoes and wine. Walter was impressed with the vast wilderness, the abundance of game which he compared to that which he had seen in Africa, and most of all, he was impressed with his moose. Details of his moose are chronicled in another story called "The Moose That Nearly Got Away."

The next morning we enjoyed a beautiful flight to the lodge. The leaves of the dwarf birch had turned from summer green to a striking vermillion punctuated by the golden leafed cottonwoods. When we saw especially beautiful scenes, I flew some lazy loops with the super cub to allow Walter to record the technicolor wonder with his camera.

As we walked from the landing strip to the lodge, my guest whooped for joy! He expressed his relief, astonishment, and approval of the appearance and comforts of the remote structure. He told me that after sharing the rude sod house accommodations I use in town, he expected something of similar quality. He was surprised to find the lodge to be far more than just a dry camp. And, he said, it smelled so nice there. As we strode over the tundra, the Hudson Bay Tea released it's pleasant

Walter and his beautiful moose.

aromas, adding to the wonder of it all. It was an ideal introduction to Trail Creek.

Chris was out hunting with my Assistants, so I busied myself with getting dinner ready to stick in the oven before Walter and I set off for a couple of hours of fishing.

Upon the other fellows' return, my assistant, Tom, took me aside to tell me that he had not been able to locate any mature rams. He and Joe had counted over one hundred Dall sheep, but only twelve were rams and the best of those would barely make a full curl. I reminded him that we were in pursuit of Grizzlies, Moose, Caribou, Sheep and Wolves, with Wolverine as a possibility, so we should just keep hunting and looking. Trail Creek valley normally held a smorgasbord of species and plenty of individual animals of each type. We just had to find them.

The weather remained unseasonably warm and the big game was not moving much. Willow Ptarmigan were coming off the North Slope in flocks numbering in the hundreds to thousands of birds which brightened the outlook for all of us. The guests told me that such high quality wing shooting was a separate activity in Europe and very costly. They were happy to enjoy the bird hunting with me and my dog, Max, at no extra cost. But, as our guests enjoyed their trip, my two assistant guides were getting nervous at the paucity of big game.

The morning of September first began clear and cooler with a slight breeze from the north, which is usually a good sign. Caribou characteristically walk with their tails, rather than their noses to the wind, so I reasoned that we would soon be seeing large groups coming off the North Slope and right down our alley, the valley of Trail Creek.

Shortly after dinner that evening as I scanned the valley from the window with the "long eye" spotting scope, a dark brown Grizzly showed up just a bit over a mile from the lodge. The brothers flipped a coin and Chris called it, giving him first option to shoot, so we all five struck off to the moguls on the east side of the valley to intercept the bear.

The wind was still from the north and in that area a steady breeze seldom carries odors to lower elevations. This prompted us to climb above the level of the bear. We had occasional glimpses of the bruin as it moved through the willow thickets below us, then we lost visual contact for more than an hour. Expecting a quick resolution to the stalk, the guests had not dressed for a prolonged exposure to the chilling wind, so we returned to the lodge.

Light was fading fast, but from inside, Tom, Joe and I all kept an anxious vigilance out the windows, still hoping to get a crack at the bear. We were focused on the side hills where we had last seen the critter when a movement just below the kitchen window caught my eye. It was the bear! I motioned to everyone to be quiet and signaled Chris to come to me. When he got to the window the bear was rubbing its back on the door frame below us and not visible, but we all could hear him quite clearly. I whispered to Chris to get his rifle, but with utmost silence as his firearm was hanging on the wall inside the entrance - a mere three feet from the bear's position and the slightest noise would surely be detected by the animal. I told Chris to take all the time he needed, but go slowly and to not even breath loudly. I motioned for the other three men to remain absolutely motionless.

As Chris crept down the stairs with the speed of a crippled snail, I remained at the window. The bear, apparently having satisfied its itchy backside, walked into clear view and turned down the trail toward the runway. At the wooden can crusher, just fifteen feet from the lodge door, the Grizzly paused and sniffed the device, perhaps detecting a residual odor, then it bit the lower arm, tearing an inch thick chunk from the four by four. Spitting out the wood, the bear looked around, lowered its head and walked toward the meat pole. It seemed to be evaluating or remembering things. The bear was completely at ease and in no great hurry to depart. It must have been aware of the presence of humans and was far too comfortable around the buildings, in my estimation. "Cabin bears" such as this one become bolder and bolder and eventually must be killed. In this case, we had a willing hunter, fully licensed and ready to do the deed.

Chris joined me at the window with his rifle in hand. The bear walked to the meat pole and studied it as if expecting a tasty treat … perhaps it had done so in the past.

Willow branches partially obscured our view of the bruin. No chance for a clear shot came to Chris.

This bear acted like he owned the place. Finding nothing of further interest, he ambled on past the burn barrel and disappeared into the willows.

I told the other three men and my dog to stand by the windows, but they should not leave the building unless I called them. With no clear view of the bruin, Chris and I eased out the door and as our feet touched the ground, I heard a rattle from a metal windbreak at the barbecue fire pit. That pinpointed the bear's location. As I carefully, slowly, chambered a cartridge, I nodded at Chris to do the same, then put my rifle on safe. Slowly I moved forward with Chris at my heels. As we passed the burn barrel we could hear the unmistakable sounds of the beast's teeth tearing at the metal windbreak.

Still wearing our house slippers and watching where we placed our feet, our steps were as silent as our ever lengthening shadows. A Gray Jay landed near us, but maintained its silence as it watched us.

Gradually, as we crept along, the form of the bear became more discernible through the willows. At twenty meters, as the bear shifted position offering a quartering shot I took a hold on Chris' sleeve, brought him alongside me, and nodded my head, indicating that he should shoot. After a few prolonged seconds, the report of Chris' eight millimeter shattered the stillness. I saw the impact of the bullet and it appeared ideal. The bear took off like a furry missile into the willows and was gone before the noise of the shot subsided. He ran straight ahead. Had he come in our direction, he would have been to us in less than two seconds. A profound silence followed the fading echo of the rifle shot.

In normal voice I told Chris to chamber another round. I heard the lodge door open as the others poured out into the chill evening air.

Max rushed directly to me, looking up anxiously for a command. I told him to heel.

Each man carried his weapon, so when they reached us I cautioned them to check that their rifles were on safe and to remain silent.

It was time to do nothing but listen intently for a few minutes. The Jay bird had flown away at the sound of the rifle, but it turned back toward us and hovered over the brush about thirty yards from our position. I told Chris that I expected to find his bear lying dead just beneath the bird.

Anxiety is a frequent visitor in times like that and everyone was itching to go after the bear, but I whispered to Joe to walk down the trail toward the runway in case the bear emerged from the brush and appeared in the open swamp. I told him to holler if he caught sight of the bruin, but not to shoot unless it appeared that the bear would escape. I sent Tom back to the lodge, told him to open the kitchen window, stand there and holler if he saw the bear.

About five minutes after Chris' shot I took the two brothers to the bear's last known position, pointed to a splotch of blood a few feet in the direction of its exit route and from there we could see the dark, motionless form of the grizzly.

We moved around to look at the animal from the front and I noted that its eyes were open and no sign of breathing movement was evident. I tossed a rock which hit the carcass on the head, eliciting no response, so I hollered to all that the bear was dead.

Chris and his first Alaskan trophy.

Chris was an experienced hunter and had held well below the midline of the bear's chest, placing his bullet just behind the right foreleg and passing through the rib cage and heart before shattering the left humerus and lodging just beneath the skin on the left shoulder. The bear was dead before he hit the ground, but still capable of doing great damage to anything it might encounter in the few seconds remaining before its final collapse.

We each took a leg and moved the carcass to the lodge yard and skinned it by lantern light.

So ended the opening day of Grizzly season.

Short strings of caribou began coming down the valley the next day which kept everyone alert and on the lookout for big bulls, which normally bring up the tail end of the first strings of southward moving caribou. Dall rams were visible daily from the lodge but none were much more than legal. Walter and I had seen plenty of mature bull moose, so I decided to take Chris back to town, then set out with the float plane to try to find a big moose for him. Joe, Tom and Walter could hunt from the lodge until we returned.

The moose hunting turned out to be excellent and Chris took one of the finest moose I had ever seen. It wound up receiving the award for number two moose in the statewide competition that year. It's story is

Chris and his award winning moose.

detailed in another tale, but its photo on the previosu pages shows what an outstanding trophy it was.

After only four days Chris and I were back at Trail Creek, however no more animals had been taken.

One clear morning we all started up the creek to check out some of the side canyons to the north for caribou, rams, and another grizzly,

We passed Break Ankle Canyon and continued on to Current Creek. A half mile short of the mouth of the creek we spotted a lone sheep feeding near the top of the rocky crest on the north side of the canyon. We had a long stretch of open alluvial fan to cross, which if we used it, would place us in clear sight of the ram long before we could gain the cover of the willows near the stream, so I slowed the pace and told everyone to line up directly behind me in hopes of presenting a single silhouette. We went only a few steps, then stopped to allow me to glass the sheep. The sheep was grazing and not aware of our presence. With our progress slowed by the frequent stops we inched across the open area.

As the sun struck the sheep my binoculars confirmed that it was a very heavy horned ram of well more than a curl, even though both sides were heavily broomed off. This was a world class ram and the best I had seen for several years. Who could guess where it had been for the past ten days or so?

Chris had taken the last animal, so now it was Walter's turn.

We five men stayed in a tight column and slowly headed for the creek. Once in the cover of the willows I sent Chris with Joe and Tom down Current Creek with instructions to stay in the brush until they could no longer see the ram, then turn back toward the base of the mountain and continue on up country, carefully checking each canyon they came to.

Walter, Max, and I walked directly up the bottom of Current Creek and through the narrow gorge that provided its exit from the high country. It was a slippery route over the stream polished, moss covered boulders, but that was a necessary inconvenience if we were to have a chance at that ram, which by then was lying on a prominent bluff, and looking our way.

After struggling through two hairpin turns filled with a clutter of slippery, mossy boulders, uprooted willows, and bordered by sheer walls we again had the ram in view. He was lying with his left broadside to us, facing the main valley to our left.

One step at a time and in close tandem, we slowly proceeded through the open space until we were concealed by the base of the hill beneath the ram. Another steep sided gully led up the mountain that would allow us to close most of the distance to the sheep without being seen.

Nearly two and a half tension filled hours had passed since we parted company with the others and Walter's anxiety had peaked. He wanted to charge quickly up the rocky chute before the sheep decided to move again, but I cautioned him to stay cool, that we should proceed at a deliberate, but cautious pace. Midday was approaching and the ram was apt to remain where he was for some time yet, unless we disturbed him. If we spooked this old ram, we would not likely ever see him again. Minutes later, Walter took a tumble, his rifle struck a rock and he barked his shin.

"Oooo, Jake, the widder (German for ram) will hear it," Walter gasped.

I motioned "shussh" and whispered to him that I doubted the noise made it all the way to the ram which was still over 500 meters from us. Walter wanted to take a peek, but I told him we should continue on our route and not expose any part of ourselves to check on the ram until we were higher up the chute.

As the gradient of the slope increased, so did the size of the boulders we encountered, slowing our progress, which increased Walter's foreboding that the ram would be gone. Eventually, as the gully flattened out near the top of the slope I eased up to look for the ram. The ram's bed was vacant!

Waving Walter up to join me as I motioned to be quiet, I decided that the ram had likely moved a bit further around the rocky bluff.

Exuding confidence, I nodded affirmatively that everything was okay and we should slowly proceed toward the ram's last bed. We would be completely exposed for more than a hundred yards as we crossed a shale slide, but this seemed the only reasonable route. Upon reaching the bluff, we had to choose between going up over the rocks or taking the lower path below the bluff. It's generally best to stay higher when hunting sheep, but the high road would be more noisy and bring with it the potential of dislodging rocks that would alert the ram as well as prevent us from seeing a lot of area just below the bluff, so we took the low road.

The loose shale and gravel below the bluff demanded very careful placement of each step. Eventually a basketball sized boulder broke loose and bounded down the slope, booming its way to the bottom. I heard Walter's worried groan behind me.

Fifteen minutes later when we had a view beyond the bluff, we could see that a broad gully laid between us and the next set of cliffs. At the base of the cliffs stood the ram looking away from us. We were a bit over two hundred meters from the sheep so I told Walter the estimated range, instructed him to lie down, take a rest and shoot as soon as he was ready. I told him to not be in a hurry as the ram was not alarmed. As Walter removed his back pack and settled in for the shot I had time to get my video camera and film the scene.

The shot was true and the ram bunched up, still on its feet. I knew it was hit, but I thought it best to anchor it with another bullet. Walter shot

The ram hung up in shale.

again and this time the ram's hind legs collapsed and it went over backwards and began rolling end over end down the slope. Before I could speak, Walter groaned as he said "the second shot was not normally necessary", and I agreed. The tumbling carcass gained speed and went over a small bluff, becoming airborne for at least twenty feet before hitting the rock-strewn surface. A few more rolls and it became lodged in the rocks.

Walter muttered that the horns would be ruined. I assured him that they would not be damaged.

We spent about thirty minutes carefully picking our way to the ram. Having seen the way the ram tumbled down the mountain, neither of us cared to match its descent.

The annular rings indicated this old head basher was thirteen and a half years of age which is far older than most Dall sheep ever live to be. He was in excellent condition, carrying over two inches of heavy tallow on his back, while all his teeth showed the wear expected of a mere eight or nine year old ram.

We caped the trophy for a shoulder mount and cut the carcass in two pieces to pack out as we would a caribou. I removed most of the fat to leave on the mountain for birds and before we were ready to depart, ravens and gray jays were hopping around and pecking at the tallow. That made it a great day for the birds too.

Walter and his massive ram.

As the meat cooled we remembered that we had not yet eaten our lunches, so before beginning our return to the lodge we laid back and savored the events of the day along with our sandwiches.

I was day dreaming of sheep ribs roasting on the fire pit.

Our loads felt heavy and the route was hazardously steep over a stub-toe prone path, but we labored along carefully and experienced no mishaps. After enjoying several short rests, we stopped at the mouth of Current Creek where Max alerted me to our three companions coming our way. They were moving slowly and soon I cold see the horns of a ram protruding from Chris' pack.

Two rams in one day, though not uncommon, is a joyous event.

When the others reached us we got their story. As Walter, Max, and I were slip-sliding our way through the narrow gorge the other men reached the east base of the valley and continued on to the north. When they came to the next major side drainage, Summer Creek, they spotted a band of eight caribou feeding on a slope about a mile up the canyon. About a half mile from the main valley that creek opens up into a large basin. The three men proceeded up toward the basin. As they rounded a bend they saw three mature rams high, near the north west rim of the basin which they would have missed had they not gone to check out the caribou. By climbing up the most southerly branch of the creek they could get above the sheep, stay out of sight as they traveled through the rimrocks to within easy range just

Joe, with the second ram of the day and Chris.

above the rams. After nearly three hours they peered over the crest to see the rams lying contentedly below them at less than one hundred yards.

No ram was clearly distinguishable as better than the others, so Chris selected one and squeezed off a shot. The ram dropped its head and was stone dead in its bed from a shot in the back of the neck. The other rams stood up, looked around and remained in place for several minutes before one moved to his dead companion and nudged him with his nose. The second ram did the same and the two stood for a few minutes, then, seemingly unconcerned, they walked off and over the rim, headed back into Trail Creek.

In telling the stories of the day we learned that Chris had shot his ram at precisely the same time as Walter took his. We heartedly congratulated one another and continued back to the lodge. Passing through a dense willow patch midway to the lodge we were joined by three Gray Jays, one of which landed on my back pack to peck at the exposed tallow and meat as I walked.

I figured that we could afford to indulge our winged fellow travelers a few beaks full of the finest meat in the world, but the birds pecked only at the remaining tallow.

Me, Max and Joe with Chris's bull.

Then as so often happens, the caribou came en masse. At first light the next morning we were amazed to see hundreds of caribou slowly grazing as they moved down stream on both sides of the valley.

With only minimal walking and waiting, but high excitement for all present, both brothers soon had a decent bull on the ground.

So we now were left with three days to hunt before the new guest hunters were scheduled to arrive and the brothers were scheduled to head back to West Germany. Each hunter had taken a Moose, Dall Ram, and Caribou, but we still had a good Grizzly to locate for Walter.

We all started down country to hunt the Popple Creek area.

I've always preferred mixed bag bookings in the fall because we typically encounter several species, but when all the tags are filled but one, we find ourselves the objects of 'Murphy's Luck', and old Murphy seldom misses a lick.

East Bowl Creek is less than a mile from the lodge and we found a dandy bull moose feeding unmolested on the succulent new willow shoots near the mouth of the drainage. We passed by without revealing our presence. The moose continued his feeding undisturbed. Plenty of caribou, including some large bulls, made themselves available on that trek, and there was a limit of

Each of the brothers got a respectable Caribou.

five per person, but the brothers decided that one caribou apiece was enough, so we moved on. Most Germans thought of caribou as they did reindeer, which are domesticated in Europe - and therefore much less appealing.

We climbed to the South Overlook and glassed for more than an hour until we located a bear on the far side of Popple Creek. The blond Grizzly was slowly moving across the slope, feeding on blue and cranberries as it moved. With a mile and a quarter of knee wrenching shin tangle to get through before we could reach the cottonwoods lining the creek, we hustled as fast as we could. The air was a chilly notch or two below freezing, but half way through the pucker brush I stopped to shed my down filled liner and stuff it into my pack.

It's always a good idea to avoid sweating in cold weather because when you inevitably slow down, if you're sweaty, the chill will really get to you. I had learned that my first year in the Arctic. My four companions were impatient with my brief pause and left all their warm clothes on. The guys were so hot to trot they were nearly jumping up and down, so we soon were once again fighting our way through the frustrating dwarf birch.

The hillside where we had seen the bear was wrinkled by multiple shallow drainages which temporarily hid the bruin as it traveled across the slope, but the bear continued to reappear as he crossed over the higher points. As we stood at the far edge of Popple creek the bear turned downhill toward us. This was very much to our advantage. An ancient glacier had deposited large mounds of debris and some huge erratics (boulders seemingly in odd places) between us and the bear, so we waited for the grizzly to emerge on our side, but after entering the broken country, it never showed itself again. For more than two hours we tried to locate our quarry, but we lost this *Ursus horribilis disappearicus*.

It had looked like a sure thing for us when the critter turned our way and how we missed seeing it again was a mystery, but such is the way of hunting.

As the sun descended behind the peaks we all began to feel cold. I cheerfully put my warm liner back on, but the others had to endure their sweaty dampness as we headed back toward the lodge.

With over five miles to cover I set a moderate pace to avoid having to travel too far in the dark as well as to help warm up my shivering companions.

Joe holding Walter's wolf.

We came to Trail Creek and before dropping off the cut bank onto the gravel, we looked once again for the bear, but saw nothing. I turned my head back to the creek and saw a grey wolf coming our direction as it loped down an open stretch of gravel on the east bank of the creek. The lobo was glancing over its shoulder repeatedly as it continued toward us, apparently preoccupied with something behind it. I motioned to the group to get down and for Walter to get ready to shoot. At a hundred and fifty meters range I told my guest to shoot. The shot caused the big wolf to drop on its chin. It was a prime adult male and pleased Walter immensely.

An overcast sky with a fierce wind developed from the North making the walk back up creek just plain miserable with stinging bits of sleet that felt like needles as they struck our reddened cheeks. We felt lucky that the weather had not been like this from the beginning and throughout the hunt.

The next December we learned that Walter's ram and Chris' moose each took second place in their category of the annual Big Three Competition.

The brothers sent their trophies to the best known taxidermist in West Germany, Wolfgang Shenk, who told them it was the best mixed bag collection from Alaska that he had ever seen.

We soon bid goodbye to the brothers, but we visited them several times on our subsequent trips to Germany.

Mac, Will, Max and Me

In 1988 I was spending part of the winter in Tucson, Arizona. A local taxidermist referred a fellow to me who wanted to hunt a Dall ram. We set the dates for the first part of the season which opened August 10. The hunter, Mac, would arrive in Kotzebue on August 8 and he informed me that he needed to return to Arizona as soon as he took his ram. He was in the construction business and needed to be on hand for some critical issues connected with a big job he was doing, but this fellow had his priorities straight and was not going to let work interfere with his hunting. He had been drawn for a Grizzly permit for that season also, but wanted to hunt sheep first, which did not require a drawing permit. He would return after a couple of weeks to pursue the bear. His big project could be scheduled to allow for these absences. He was the boss, which helped.

When Mac arrived the wind and weather were amenable for a shot straight up to the lodge, so we loaded the cub and were off. A big blow was forecast to come in, so it was good that we got out before the storm hit. Storm force winds in the mountains are not a cheery prospect when flying in a small airplane. Once this low pressure system arrived we might be grounded for several days. Its preferable that grounded days are spent at the lodge, as hunting is still possible.

Teresa and I had been keeping track of two dandy rams on the west side of Trail Creek and a large single ram had been showing itself on the east side. I was hopeful that Mac and I would have a good quick hunt, allowing him to get back to Arizona to see to his project.

But Murphy had other plans for us, as it turned out.

The first night at the lodge a gale force wind of about forty miles per hour and higher gusts began to howl down the valley. The blow matured into freight train winds of storm force ferocity and velocity (fifty-five miles per hour or higher) and brought along a driving rain.

We were all thankful to be in the lodge with the aircraft secured. I had buried old automobile tires about two thirds of the way into the ground, leaving the top third of the tires exposed for attaching tie down ropes. They were strong enough to resist the strongest of blows - in fact those old tires were probably stronger than the tie-down ropes or the aircraft wing components.

It was so good to not be flying in the conditions that had developed.

By mid afternoon the next day the rain was diminishing and the winds, apparently having grown tired, were puffing along at a mere fifteen miles per hour. Mac, Max and I set out for the North Overlook. Midway to our intended goal we heard a wolf howl, then we spotted a large gray wolf on the alluvial delta across the creek. The animal was trotting to the north and kept on going. I figured, due to the single howl, that he was rejoining his pack.

Mac said he would like to shoot a wolf and I assured him that I would like that too. We always offered the first wolf to our guests at no charge, but they would have to use a metal locking tag on any animal they shot. Mac had elected to not purchase a wolf tag, as he could use a more expensive caribou tag on a wolf, if he got a lobo. The issue of using a more expensive caribou or sheep tag on a wolf did not bother Mac. But no opportunity came for a shot.

In Alaska a hunter can use a species tag for an animal on any other species for which the tag costs the same or less.

We kicked up several coveys of Willow Ptarmigan, but we were carrying only our rifles. We figured that some evening we would collect some "wild chicken" closer to the lodge.

Moose sign was thick and we glassed about fifteen *Alces gigas* that afternoon. The bulls were all carrying velvet on their still growing antlers and were very tolerant of each other this early in the season. They would begin to shed the velvet sometime between August 17 and September 5 and the amity between the bulls would be shed along with the velvet antler covering.

We counted only forty-three sheep on our hike and none were mature rams. It seemed the big wind had blown our three good rams away. But I was confident they had not gone far.

In hope of locating the two old rams we had seen on the west side, we struck off toward West Bowl the next morning. Immediately we spotted some sheep that we had not seen the day before. Unfortunately none were rams old enough to shoot. We made a long day of it and returned to the lodge as the rain began.

Another day inside was called for. Everyone got a nice nap and after supper the rain ended. We hoped for a good day in the morning.

Our hopes were met with a clear day with little wind. Max was excited as we walked toward the East Bowl and the big cirque basin at the base of a particularly rough mountain we called Aconcagua. I wanted to check the deep, rough chimneys and canyons on the east aspect of the mountain - the far side - an area we could not see from the lodge, and seldom visited due to the distance, but it was prime summer sheep habitat, and Mac was a good walker.

We found plenty of fresh sheep tracks and droppings, but sighted only ewes and lambs. When we topped out at the cirque basin, plenty of sign encouraged us to continue through the steep, rough back side of Aconcagua. That aspect of the mountain formed an escarpment of extraordinary cliffs and chimneys, which, along with its distance from the lodge, is why we seldom hunted there. Previously some of my guests had refused to try to walk and climb through the hazardous terrane, but Mac was not bothered by the physical demands or risks of the prospect.

The steep gulches and ledges required very slow, careful walking. I was concerned that we would either walk by sheep directly beneath us that we could not see due to the vertical cliffs or that we would top out of a gulch and find ourselves too close to sheep that were not visible until the last minute. We spent over four hours in the rough stuff before encountering a band of five mature bull Caribou on a small saddle at the far end of the rugged back side of the mountain. These Caribou all still carried velvet on their impressive antlers. We had yet to see a single ram.

The saddle gave us a wonderful panorama of that stretch of the DeLong Mountains. We kicked back and enjoyed a sandwich before continuing around the north side of the mountain, which would lead us back into East Bowl Creek.

As we were traversing the last of the rocky chimneys I glanced up and saw the ram. He was lying on a promontory casually watching us. We were about five or six hundred yards below the ram and he had us clearly in sight. He was past a full curl and broomed on the right horn.

What to do? It was a taker sheep for sure, but too far to shoot and with us spotted, it surely would not allow us to approach close enough to try a shot.

I told Mac that we and Max should go back to the last gulch and all disappear from the ram's view. Then, after a few minutes, Max and I would emerge for the ram to clearly see us. We would just move about aimlessly to hold the sheep's attention, but not threaten him. Mac would have to go up the gulch alone and try to get even with or above the resting ram. If he could get close enough for a shot, he should take it.

In my experience, it seems that animals do not count. This has been borne out several times in circumstances similar to those we encountered with this ram.

Max, my Labrador, was anxious. He kept looking from me to the ram and seemed to wonder why we were not going for the sheep. I spent a lot of our time just petting my dog and quietly talking to him.

After an interminable wait, we heard the report of Mac's rifle, and the echo as it reverberated through the canyons. The old ram struggled to rise, but abruptly stumbled and came rolling down the rocky slide toward us. As the carcass began to slow down, one horn got hung up in the rocks and the dead ram was anchored.

Mac had his sheep and time enough to get back to his job. It was a really good day, that thirteenth day of August.

Mac, the ram, and Max.

The pack back to the lodge was easy with Mac and I splitting the load. We reached the camp just before midnight and hit the sack, planning an early departure for Kotzebue the next morning. I would remove the skull from the cape, flesh and salt it when I returned to Trail Creek, as Mac was winging it home on the jet.

Max, Teresa and I had a few days with no guests at Trail Creek. We spent the next week doing small jobs at the lodge and just enjoying the unspoiled wilderness. Caribou began to drift down the drainage, so I shot two bulls for winter meat. The caribou were beginning to shed their temporary antler covering as they thrashed willows to remove the shreds of hanging velvet.

With such nice weather we flew over to the Kivalina River for some superb Arctic Char fishing. Another day was spent at Feniak Lake, fishing for Lake Trout and photographing the impressive pre-historic rock and sod dwellings near the lake shore. Max accompanied us on all the trips. He enjoyed sitting on Teresa's lap and gazing out the windows as we flew. Teresa didn't complain ... too much.

Max and the Lake Trout seem to be having a discussion.

As always, the time went by much too quickly. Soon it was time for me to make a trip to Kotzebue to freeze the meat we had hanging and meet the incoming hunter.

The new guest was an Iowa farmer named Willard. He told me of how he had started life on his family farm, near my birthplace, Fairfield, bought more ground, was successful and branched out into other businesses. Will did not have a lot of formal schooling, but he had more than the usual amount of smarts. Field smarts, rather than street smarts they were, in his case.

He had made time to indulge some of his hobbies such as Indian artifact collecting which he became interested in when he noticed arrowheads in the dirt he disked up prior to planting his corn fields. Another driving passion of Will's was hunting. He had plenty of white tailed deer, pheasants, rabbits and other wild game on his farms and preferred their meat to that of domestic animals. That's unusual for a farmer! For decades before I met him, he had been traveling to western states to hunt elk and mule deer.

Will lived nearby a cousin of mine named Alice, who had come up to cook at the lodge in 1986. She highly recommended that Will make a trip to Alaska and she told me he was eager to do so. I rarely made any calls to people soliciting their hunting business unless they have personally contacted me first, but I made an exception in this case and I was glad that I did.

When I met Will at the Alaska Airlines terminal he impressed me as being a truly good old boy. He was about six feet three inches tall and carried not an ounce of fat. At seventy-six years of age, Will appeared to be as fit as most marines just out of boot camp. Additionally, he was a humble man and delightful company.

We flew directly to the lodge after storing Will's travel clothes and hard gun case at my little sod shack in Kotzebue.

After we got Will situated in the bedroom of his choice I set him up to check his rifle. He was using a Winchester Model 70 chambered in .338 magnum. It shot spot on.

We enjoyed a big supper of chicken fried caribou steaks, mashed potatoes and gravy, salad, and a fresh baked apple pie. Will commented that it was a farm boy's dinner - and his favorite type.

Normally I am awake well before daylight and far earlier than our guests, but the next morning when I quietly left my bedroom to brew a pot of coffee, Will was looking out the window. He told me that he was pretty certain that he had seen some animals moving on the hillside two hundred yards from the lodge, but couldn't tell for sure what they were or how many were in the bunch. I thought to myself, for this guy, as the song goes - "in the fields of opportunity, it's plowing time again." He was as enthusiastic a guest hunter as I have ever enjoyed spending time with.

As daylight found its way to the valley we could see caribou in all quadrants. Will told me that to him, they all looked big, but he had read some articles about the deer of the tundra and realized that many first time caribou hunters shoot too soon and end up with a mediocre bull. He wanted me to point out a really outstanding head.

This old boy had done his homework.

Seeing nothing worthy of closer inspection, we had a big breakfast, Teresa packed our lunches and we headed north with Max at my left heel.

The valley's resident Willow Ptarmigan population had burgeoned to hundreds of birds, some in flocks of thirty or forty. The ptarmigan were changing to white plumage, showing their mottled, random beauty. Will said he wanted to get some of those beautiful things to eat and a pair to have mounted, but he said he would not shoot any birds until he had a caribou on the ground.

Max couldn't understand why we ignored the provocative birds, but he did not stray from my side.

Caribou were coming down both sides of Trail Creek in long strings made up of mostly cows and calves with a few young bulls in the mix.

We paused at the mouth of Current Creek to have a sandwich and do some serious glassing. Sheep were again on both sides of the creek and nine of the fifty-two animals we scrutinized were rams. Will told me that he would like to go after a sheep sometime.

Another mile up the drainage we came onto a trio of big Caribou bulls, one of which was clearly the best of the bunch and the best I had seen that season. The animals were slowly grazing on the lichens and sedges in the open tundra. We sneaked to beneath a high cut bank and then went as rapidly as possible to come up adjacent to the feeding bulls and downhill at about one hundred fifty yards. As we peered over the edge, Max crawled along with us, dragging his belly over the vegetation.

Will with his big bull trophy loaded and Max looking on.

I told Will to chamber a round and take the largest bull. With slow deliberation, Will settled in and fired. The bull dropped immediately and did not struggle. He killed it dead on its feet.

Will was pleased with his trophy, which he said was bigger than any elk he had ever seen. He preferred a European skull mounting, so we did not keep the cape. I carried the meat out and we took our time heading back to the lodge.

Unfortunately Will had not agreed to me submitting an application for a Grizzly Permit for him the previous spring. Of course, that insured that we would encounter several dandy bears - and it happened just that way.

The four quarters, back straps, ribs and heart of Will's caribou were left hanging on the meat pole. The scent of the fresh meat wafted down the valley, borne by the north wind. It was a clear and unmistakeable invitation to bears.

As we sipped the first taste of fresh coffee the following morning Will said he saw an animal down off the far end of the runway. We all took binoculars to the window and after locating the critter I identified it as a very large bear. The bruin was scratching about in the stream side gravel, digging masue, or Eskimo potatoes - a thin tuber favored by mountain bears in their Autumn foraging.

Using the tripod mounted sixty power spotting scope, we could see bits of the root hanging from the corners of the bear's mouth, as it voraciously devoured the delicacy. As the animal came nearer it stuck its head in the air and obviously became interested in what its nose told him lay ahead. It had smelled the fresh meat. After pausing several times to lift its head and zero in on the temptation it sensed, the bear stood up on its hind legs momentarily, then dropped to its feet and began to run toward the lodge.

"Oh, that's a big one, Jake. I sure wish I had a permit," moaned Will.

How I wished he had allowed me to make an application for him, but instead of mentioning that, I reminded Will that it was not yet open season for bears. We were a few days short of September one. That took away part of the sting of Will's decision to not apply for a permit.

The galloping Grizzly slowed to a fast walk about four hundred yards from the lodge, then it paused. Once again it stood on its hind legs to see better. When it dropped to all fours, it turned ninety degrees and jaunted east into the moguls, where it laid down.

This bear seemed to be familiar with the lodge and smells associated with human occupancy. The lure of the meat did not override the old boar's caution. Big bears don't get big and old by being careless … or overly bold with people.

After half an hour the bear rose and walked up the hills into East Bowl, enjoying the lush blueberries as he went.

We did nothing to disturb the bear, in hopes that it might be around when season opened and Mac might have an opportunity to take it.

After breakfast a large flight of ptarmigan landed just in front of the lodge. Ptarmigan are usually predictable. We decided to approach a flock from down wind. When we were very close, some of the birds would run ahead, but a few would rise and headed into the breeze, provide us with ideal wing shooting opportunities. So Will and I, with Max's assistance, soon had sixteen birds to skin and butcher for dinner. Will wanted to have a brace mounted, but I told him we should hold off on that until closer to his time of departure.

Teresa had been keeping her eyes on the bear as Will and I were shooting. She said the bear did not react to the shooting.

It turned out to be a lucky thing that Will took his caribou when he did, as the steady stream of southward migrating animals slowed to a trickle and for the rest of the season we saw no bulls to equal the one he killed.

That evening shortly before dark we glassed two more single bears on opposite sides of the canyon. Will remarked that it seemed like he had landed on the planet of the bears.

A Ptarmigan Telegraph message on the KOTZ radio told me that Mac would be in on the next day's evening jet, so I loaded the hanging, aged meat and flew the cub in to pick him up.

September first, opening day of grizzly season, would be upon us the day after the next.. We saw many big bull moose, some of which had already shed their antler velvet, leaving their massive headgear white, with some bloody spots. At a distance the antlers stood out like headlights on a car, but larger - in some cases they looked more like two sheets of plywood. We had little extra time for the trip or I would have flown around more to get a feel for the caribou situation, but we did see groups of dozens of the tundra deer on our direct route to camp. Eight miles south of the lodge we flew over three large gray wolves lying on the tundra. The canines paid no attention to the airplane. They did not even get up.

Mac and I landed at the lodge strip just at dark. I wanted to focus the next day on trying to locate the huge bear we had seen so close to home a few days before.

None of the three Grizzlies we glassed near the lodge had come for the hanging meat, to my relief. First of all, I wanted to eat that meat with my family and share some with friends. Secondly, once a bear becomes brave enough to come close to a cabin, it becomes bolder and bolder, until in nearly every case, eventually it must be killed. If one came anytime after three o'clock the next morning, it could be legally shot. If it was not the giant bear, I would run it off, as I had done with dozens of bears over the past quarter of a century.

Wouldn't you know it? The next morning we saw no game except for ptarmigan. We three men walked with Max following, north toward the

The top of the "bear stairs."

head of Trail Creek. We paused at Current Creek to scrutinize the area from the "bear stairs."

For decades, maybe centuries, bears had been walking up the ridge on the north side of Current Creek, placing their feet in the same place, which resulted in an easily seen trail of depressions up to six inches deep, leading up toward a large boulder. We had located a large sleeping bear lying with its back against the boulder on three previous occasions and had collected the bear, shooting each as it lay in its bed.

In my view, shooting a bear or any other animal in its bed is no disgrace, - its not like "ground sluicing" birds - it merely confirms the efficiency and care of the stalk, but this day, the boulder had no hairy tenant.

Any lone boulder, tree, or other outstanding feature in a wild landscape attracts bears. Often they scratch themselves on the rough aspects, leaving long hairs. They commonly defecate close by. Most such prominences show signs of bears bedding nearby. Many show signs of paw prints as seen at the bear stairs. Cabins also attract bruins. The ground around our lodge and other cabins show deeply indented bear footprints made over decades of visits by bears.

The day was sunny, calm, and insect free, providing an irresistible opportunity for a leisurely nap on the hillside after we consumed our sandwich. I slipped my hip boots off. Will, at first a bit itchy to get walking, soon was snoring. Mac, in sleep deficit from the demands of the big job and the flight back to Kotzebue, dozed off. Max was stretched out in ecstasy and sleeping soundly, occasionally twitching as if from a bad dream. I was about to nod off when I saw a large brown animal moving down Trail Creek. I noticed it briefly in the willows near the stream, but soon lost sight of it. I concentrated my binocular stare on the area and picked up glimpses of the brown body and noticed individual bushes moving. There was no wind, so an animal was causing the bush movement. When the beast stepped out into a small open spot, I knew it was the great bear we saw a few days before, or another of similar size and color.

Silently I nudged Mac who came awake with a start.

"I think we have a big bear coming our way buddy," I whispered.

Mac sat bolt upright and asked where the bear was. The bear would disappear for several minutes before once again revealing its location, most often by disturbing the bushes it was passing through.

We woke Will and gathered up our gear. I put my boots back on as we started down off the hill.

"Kin I go too, or do you want me to stay here?" Will asked.

I told him we should all go, but we must maintain complete silence and be ready to hunker down if I gave the hand signal.

With such a critical need of silence, I told Mac to put a round into the chamber, put the safety on, and make sure his magazine was full. He might be shooting at very close quarters. I told Will to load up, also. I put one up the spout, as well. Our magazines were fully loaded as always when hunting.

Given the lay of the land, it seemed our best chance to not miss the bear would be by following the open gravel of Current Creek as it coursed toward the main drainage. The bear might sense us and turn back into the brush, but if we were in the bushes, it could continue on its present course and cross the creek unseen by us. Having good visibility is paramount in all hunting and often requires compromises in dense, brushy situations.

We walked slowly in file, forming one silhouette and I reminded all to avoid disturbing rocks and other noises. Mac was just behind me and Will was last in line. Max walked at my left heel.

As we neared the mouth of Current Creek I wondered if we would see the bear again. Then, I caught an unmistakable glimpse of its long brown hair as the bruin struggled to bring up a root of masue. I motioned "down" for all. Then I waved Mac to creep up on my right side. Max leaned against my left leg.

The bear kept its back to us for a few moments before turning to come up the side of the creek directly toward us. This old bear seemed familiar with the lay of the land and the creek bed. It was completely unaware of our presence only sixty yards away.

"Shoot him in the chest," I whispered to Mac.

The bear raised its head and looked our way just as Mac fired.

Mac's bullet struck the bear below the chin and it rolled over. It did not twitch at all.

With Max anxiously wagging his tail at my side I said "Okay, Max, hunt him up," and the dog rushed to the side of the fallen bruin, but stayed back a few feet, then cautiously eased in and began to thrust his nose into the body of the bear. This bear was as dead as the river rocks it laid upon..

Two happy hunters and my dog, poking the bear.

This was about as big a bear as inland Grizzlies ever get. His teeth showed wear indicating an age of well over twenty years. His hair was thick and the guard hairs were long and silky. We were all ecstatic with Will's superb trophy bear. It placed number two in the annual statewide competition.

And it was not yet mid afternoon. What a day!

We had no need to be in a hurry. We refilled our water jugs at the creek, kicked around the rocks, and picked up some ancient coral fossils before skinning the bear. I took my time with that job, leaving as little fat as possible on the hide. This was a "sweet" bear with no objectionable odors.

Mac wanted to try bear stew, so he carried the two hinds to camp while I packed out the hide with head and paws still attached. That evening I removed the head and feet, leaving the final close fleshing for the next day.

After breakfast I sent Mac and Will to the east moguls to glass for Moose, Caribou and Wolves. Both men had decided to include more animals in this hunt. I sold Mac a moose permit, Will said he would hold off. Only bears required a drawn permit, so that made expanding the bag of most any hunt a very real and handy possibility, and many guests did buy tags for more animals after a few days into a booked hunt.

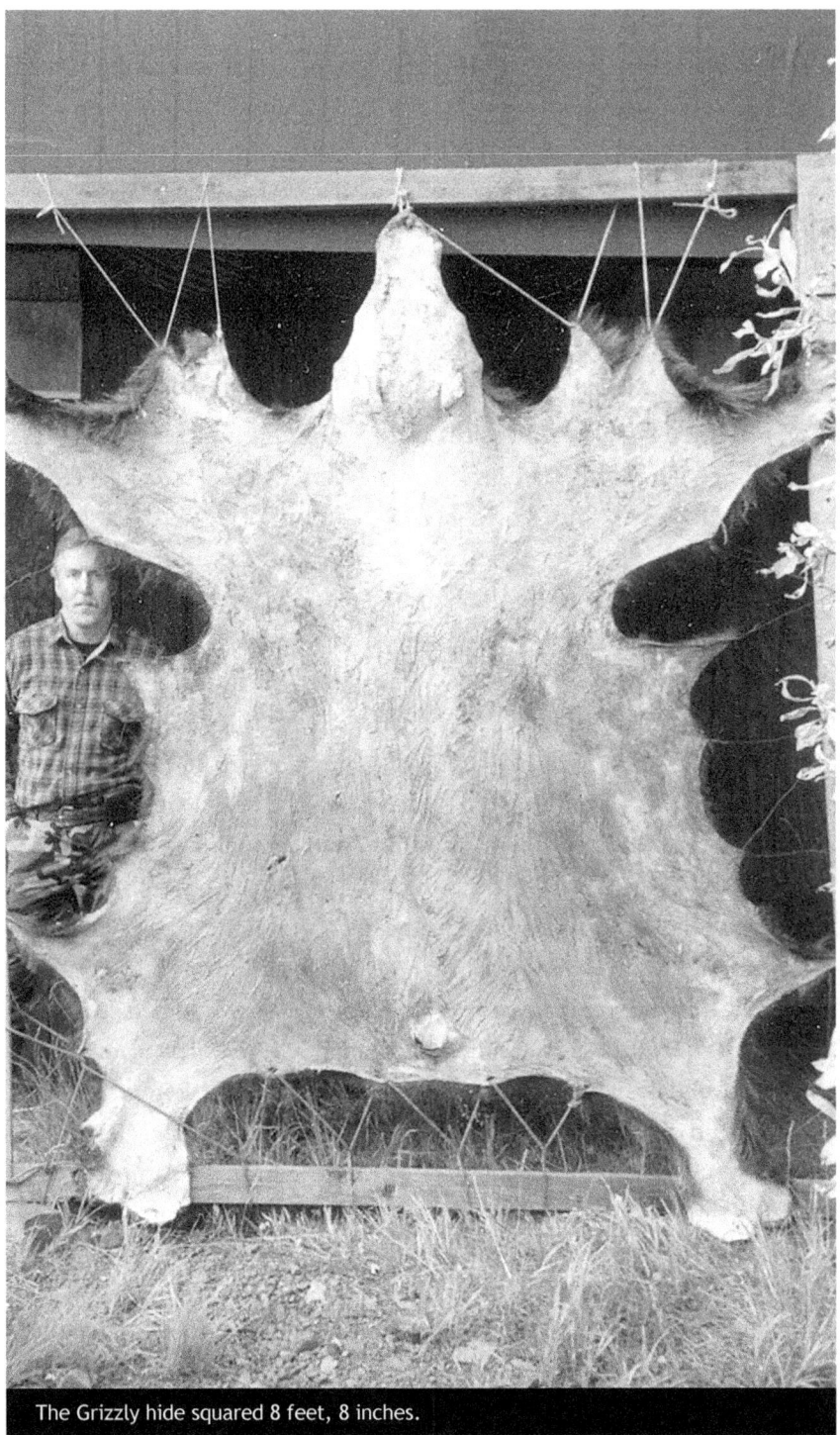

The Grizzly hide squared 8 feet, 8 inches.

It took me four hours to finalize the fleshing, then I salted the hide and let it remain skin side up until evening. The salt drew moisture from the skin which formed puddles . Before dark, Mac and I held the skin up to drain off the water, then folded it in half, skin to skin, before rolling it up and putting it into a large wash tub inside the shop. The next day I assembled the stretching frame and used wires to hang the hide.

That night we heard wolves howling from at least two different locations down the creek.

Mac said that he wanted to try to get a moose, then head back to Arizona. He had been phenomenally lucky with both his sheep and his bear, but he still had to tend to his construction business.

Will said he was a bit tired from the day before and would be happy to stay at the lodge, so off went Mac, Max, and I to see if we could locate a good bull.

We walked a fast pace to the South Overlook and before even settling in to glass the large vista before us, we spotted a huge bull nosing a cow about a mile away. We bailed off the overlook and in less than forty-five minutes were in the area we'd seen the moose. Another calm day allowed the remnant essence of moose to linger - I was sure I could smell the bull, which by now was beginning to enter the rut. The bulls urinate in a slight depression, then roll in the sticky, stinky mud to anoint themselves with their special essence. Cows are attracted to that rutty smell. I've often wondered if it would make an attractive men's cologne?

Since the willows were so dense, I did not want to try to penetrate the thicket, feeling it likely that one or the other moose would detect us, then spook and every moose in the half mile long thicket would vacate the area.

We crossed Trail Creek and set up on an old glacial esker (a long ridge of gravel and other sediment, typically having a winding course, deposited by meltwater from a retreating glacier or ice sheet) to wait for the moose to make the next move. The top of the esker put us about twenty feet above the willows providing us a good vantage point to observe the immediate region.

A cow cooperated by emitting a low mournful moan. The bull grunted and shook his antlers. We heard him before we saw the tops of his palms. The cow was between us and the bull, but the heavy brush allowed us only brief views of her body, which was always partially obscured by the dense vegetation.

We moved to the north end of the esker. The cow moaned again from further down the creek, so we hustled back to the south extreme of the esker.

This cow was playing hard to get with the bull. Back and forth the two huge animals traipsed through the brush. After an hour of frustrating maneuvering, finally the bull exposed himself well enough for us to get a full appreciation of his rack.

"I like it, Jake," confirmed Mac.

"Shoot him first unobstructed shot you get, Mac," I replied.

Another long wait gave us the impression that the big bull was not going to offer an opportunity, then, without any recent indication of his proximity, the bull stepped between two big willows just across the creek from us at about one hundred and twenty yards. Mac fired.

The bull staggered, but stayed on his feet.

"Shoot him again, Mac," I hollered.

Mac put two more quick shots into the confused bull before it fell. All three shots entered the right side just behind the shoulder, but none knocked the giant down. As is common for moose, this huge bull bled out internally and died on his feet.

Mac's third trophy.

We were quite a distance from the lodge - about four walking miles. We went right to work butchering the moose and headed back to the lodge, carrying only the tenderloins, back straps and heart. We cut willows to pile on the meat.

The next day we began packing the meat back to the lodge. It took four stagger loads for each of us over the next two days. Luckily no bears intervened in our meat recovery, though ravens had been at the kill site since early the first morning. We kept looking for caribou, but saw only cows and calves.

Mac said he should go back home the next day.

First thing in the morning we loaded up the bear hide, the moose rack and as much meat as we could safely carry and flew to town. Mac left most of the moose meat with me, but he took some choice cuts and some bear meat. As we flew directly to town we saw thousands of caribou, all headed south. Mac expressed a wish to hunt a big bull, but could not rationalize taking the time just then. I figured he had handled his work and time dilemma very well for that season.

Mac was able to get a seat on the plane departing that same afternoon and took his trophies and forty pounds of prime meat with him.

Considering all, I believe Mac was as lucky as any guest hunters that I have had at Trail Creek.

My new friend, Will was patiently sitting in the living room when I returned. He had collected some more ptarmigan and had them skinned and ready for Teresa to fry up for supper. This older gentleman was not the least bit anxious and told me that he had as much time as he needed to find a bull moose, and maybe one of those wolves we'd been hearing. He mentioned that he was a little sore, so I fired up the sauna and we enjoyed the therapeutic heat and relaxing benefits of that ancient means of personal hygiene and relaxation.

The next day was a splendid one for walking about. Will preferred to go up north. He purchased a moose tag and mentioned that if he saw a bull caribou better than the one he had already shot, he just might use the moose tag on a second caribou. The non resident limit of caribou was five per year.

Willow Ptarmigan were beginning to show white feathers.

So off we went, with Max at heel. Again this time we ate our sandwiches at my favored site near the bear stairs and stretched out on the tundra mattress to soak up the sunshine. I could see that what remained of the carcass of Mac's bear had been chewed on by other bears. Two ravens were nearby and had left their deposits on the shredded pile of guts. As before, Will was soon snoring. I glassed Dall sheep in small bands throughout Trail Creek and up the side canyons.

A pair of golden eagles soared above us. I have seen eagles swoop in, knock a lamb off a precipice and then land to eat the carcass, but never after early July. By mid summer, apparently the lambs are large, sturdy, and alert enough to avoid the eagles best efforts. The huge raptors soared above us, eventually flying down the valley and out of sight.

Everywhere we walked, especially near swamps, seeps and springs along the hillside we saw a confusion of lemming trails. I was reminded of the great freeway complexes in urban America. As Will snored and I glassed for game, I noticed two Marsh Hawks gliding just below us. I saw them make several dives for lemmings. On two occasions I saw the hawk carry a lemming away in its beak. No doubt the pair had nestlings to feed.

About two miles up the creek, just beneath the North Overlook I saw the momentary flash of moose palms. I remained concentrating on the spot for several minutes but I did not get a good look at the animal.

Will and I returned to the lodge after six o'clock without seeing a shootable animal, and we got to bed early.

Another lovely day greeted us in the morning. Will wanted to go north again, but he wanted to carry a 30:30 lever action carbine that I kept in camp which was a few pounds lighter than his .338. I agreed to that, as my .300 Winchester magnum would be with me, and we returned to the bear stairs. Having seen the flash of moose antlers further up the creek the day before, I suggested we continue walking. When we climbed to the top of the North Overlook, we took time for a bite to eat. Will was settling in for a nap when I saw the moose below us. Two cows were standing in an open spot surrounded by dense willows. To one side was a "mulligan" bull - a young one, perhaps fifteen months of age with its first small set of antlers. This youngster had ideas of jumping one of the mature cows, but they wanted nothing to do with the immature upstart. Then I heard the grunt of a mature bull. This fellow was a qualified contender for the attentions of the cows and he came right into the clearing to assert his dominance. As he merged from the brush he was slowly turning his antlers from right to left, making a full display of his cranial weaponry. Another bull grunted from nearby. The cows were working their ears like flag semaphores, turning their heads, listening to and evaluating the different expressions - promises maybe - of their would-be lovers.

Will said he would like to shoot the bigger bull, but I cautioned him to hold until we saw the third one. At the sight of the approaching, displaying bull, the mulligan bull wheeled around and crashed through the brush as he made his hasty escape.

We were a bit over two hundred yards from the moose, which was too far for the carbine unless absolutely necessary. I offered Will the use of my .300 Winchester Magnum, but he wanted to use "the gun that won the west" as he called it. Also, he looked forward to stalking closer.

The third bull revealed himself. His antlers were larger than the other big one, but were noticeably asymmetrical. Will decided that he wanted the smaller, more balanced and esthetically pleasing rack.

Again I offered my rifle, but Will declined. Oh well, I figured if we blew the stalk, that moose was barely okay, but not all that great, and we had time to seek another - hopefully more impressive trophy.

But Will was showing signs of tiring and wanted a moose that day, if possible.

Will and his choice of bulls with the 30:30.

We angled around to allow us to approach the moose from down wind. Just as we entered the dense undergrowth a flock of ptarmigan flushed and cackled as they flew directly over the moose.

The cows startled, but the two bulls paid no attention to the birds. The cows ran about forty yards, then turned their attention back to their two would-be suitors.

Carefully placing each foot, avoiding dead branches and moving ever so slowly, we eased our way to within sixty yards of the mob of moose. Max was walking with his side pressed to my left leg, occasionally looking up at me.

Will had a round in the chamber, when I nodded he pulled back the hammer and fired. The bull shuddered and I told Will to "shoot him again,." Three more shots had the bull on the ground.

"Yippee," shouted Will. Not one to normally show much emotion, Will was pleased with this animal. He estimated its weight at sixteen hundred pounds, which I knew was about right, having weighed some live, anesthetized bulls with the Alaska Department of Fish and Game in years past. Most guest hunters estimate the weight of their moose at much higher - more than a ton, but this old farmer knew big animals.

We were a good five miles from camp, but with the water level still low, I could return with a Honda and trailer for the bulk of the meat.

For the trip back to camp, I carried out the tenderloins, heart and one back strap. Will was showing signs of fatigue. Considering his age and the fact that he was in a new country, doing new things, I thought he was doing great.

The next day I returned with Max and the machine. The trip was easy, following the gravel banks of the main channel, which was approved by the local National Park Service superintendent in those days.

So Will had a dandy caribou and moose with several more days to hunt. We were seeing Grizzlies nearly every day, we glassed six singles one day, but couldn't hunt them without a permit. Murphy's Law was in effect, as well as the Alaska Department of Fish and Game regulations.

As I was hanging the moose meat Will told me he had glassed a good ram on the West side of Trail Creek, near a natural mineral lick. I knew the area and doubted it would be a comfortable trek for Will. I was hesitant to explain that to my guest, expecting that he would say he could do it, so I let it go unanswered.

Sometimes blessings come with such timeliness, they seem no less than miraculous.

During breakfast Teresa noticed a sheep feeding on the slope just above the bear stairs which is only about two easy miles from the lodge. I expected it was probably a ewe, but I put the spotting scope on it and was elated to see a dandy ram - and down so low! This was a hunt that I thought Will could do with ease.

Will bought the tag and we set off. This time Teresa, as well as Max accompanied us.

Wind was not a problem, but we needed to approach the ram from below which required that we sneak and in places, crawl, through dense willow thickets. At one point we paused on our knees. I turned back and saw Will standing upright, scratching his head.

"Get down, Will. The ram will see you, get down," I urged.

Will said he guessed he just forgot. His knees were bothering and he needed to stretch, so he stood up, but forgot about the ram. It must have been a touch of old timers disease - maybe just a senior moment, or a brain belch.

The ram was grazing with its rump to us and missed Will's action. I kept a closer eye on Will after that.

We spent over an hour wiggling our way up toward the base of the hill beneath the ram. The sheep was moving up hill as the morning wore on, but we found terrane to conceal our advance and after another hour we had him within reasonable range. The ram was uphill about one hundred fifty yards from us. This time, Will had his .338, but asked to use my .300. I jacked a shell into the chamber, put the safety on and told him to hold for what he wanted to hit.

"Well, its steep and straight uphill Jake, maybe I better hold a little high," was his concern.

"Will, if you hold high, you will hit high. Just aim for the thickest part of his body, right behind the shoulder, do not hold high. Holding too high is the most common error made by hunters, especially if shooting up hill. Far and away most missed shots occur because the hunter "held high" due to miscalculation of range or due to shooting uphill.

Will did as I instructed, slowly squeezed the trigger, the ram collapsed, and rolled part way down the hill toward us.

It was a beautiful ram about eight and a half years of age.

Well, we all had plenty to be thankful for and Will said the ram was the finest trophy he had ever taken.

Jake and Will with the dandy ram.

Teresa packed out the head and cape, while I carried the meat. We had less than one hour of easy walking to put us in the yard of the lodge.

We dined on sheep tenderloins and eggs the next morning, with fire roasted ribs that evening. Will spent the next two days shooting ptarmigan. He kept a nice brace of birds to have mounted for his living room back at the farm near Batavia, Iowa. He had brought along a pair of panty hose, about which I teased him, to keep the birds' feathers in good shape for his taxidermist.

Teresa accompanied us on this, her first ram hunt.

The bears must have known that they were destined to be immune to bullet lead for that season, as we continued to see at least two single adult bears each day.

Will departed a very happy man and vowed to return to hunt a Grizzly, which he did.

1989
Multiple Species Hunts after a TOUGH WINTER

The winter of 1988-1989 was a real tough one in Alaska. The big Arctic high pressure system was so strong it ran the Barometer up beyond aircraft altimeter settings. Commercial aircraft were grounded for all but daylight flights for several days in January - an extremely rare event. Snow accumulated to record depths and many new low temperature records were set at reporting stations throughout the state. Shallow lakes froze all the way to the bottom, killing most of the fish.

In November of 1988 I drove my pickup with an Alaskan camper on the back down from Kodiak to Arizona to knock around in the great southwest and maybe do some Coes and Mule deer hunting for myself. The trip down the Alcan highway was best described as just plain miserable. My dog Max and I ran into some minus thirty degree weather with roads as slick as iced glass. My 1986 four wheel drive Ford F150 had an extra long wheel base which one would expect to give it less tendency to slip, but it proved to be the end swappingest vehicle I had ever driven. I had to slow way down below normal to shepherd that machine over the slick spots and it kept my nerves in an elevated state of high twitchiness.

A friend asked me to help him with some of his hunters and I was happy to do so as I would still have time to pursue Coes deer, feral hogs and more on my own when his paying guests were long gone.

But that's another tale, or maybe three.

When people saw my Alaska license plate and the guide service magnetic logos on my truck they would invariably mention how bad they'd heard the winter was in Alaska that year. I paid attention to what was happening back home.

It stayed so cold for so long with inordinately heavy snow cover that I dreaded what the big game stocks would be looking like the coming fall and I had a pretty full book of guest hunters lined up with deposits already paid.

But we just have to play the cards we're dealt. There's nothing new about that. Worrying never does anyone any good anyway. And in the case of wild game populations, the contributing factors are many, complex, interactive and not all that well understood.

I returned to the north in late May, got the wheel plane checked out and the annual inspection done before flying it to Kotzebue. The deep freeze had prolonged the ice lock on the lakes and rivers. I went up to the lodge to find that the aufis glacier that covers the lower end of my main runway each winter had retreated sufficiently to allow me to land the super cub.

The shallow braided streams in that country freeze to the bottom, then the spring-fed water builds up and flows over the top throughout the winter adding depth to the ice cover. The increasing weight of the thickening ice compresses the lower levels, producing the pale blue color and density of true glacier ice. I discovered that high quality glacier ice lasts longer in a whiskey glass, too. It looked like I wouldn't need to fly any ice to the lodge for cocktails and to keep our groceries fresh that year, which was normal until the generalized climate warming began to be felt in the 1990s.

Aufis glacier near the end of my landing strip.

Multiple Species Hunts after a TOUGH WINTER

Max, my labrador, and I spent a week just sprucing up the buildings and enjoying the pristine wilderness which we had all to ourselves. We watched snow drifts and ice shrink for about ten days before I figured it was time to fly back to Kotzebue and then on to Fairbanks to get the other Super Cub which was on floats.

Max didn't appreciate the jet flight to Fairbanks as he had to endure the journey in a kennel, but he sure was happy to not be left behind and he was just plain ecstatic at being released when I picked him up at the baggage claim. He would sort of pinch his hind legs together and then duck walk outside as fast as possible to avoid relieving himself inside the terminal. He was as good as any dog could be. He was the best dog I ever had - absolutely.

For more than twelve years I had flown federal and state biologists for most - and some years for all - of the big game surveys in NW Alaska. I knew the procedures and reporting requirements, so I collected all of the most recent data from the Alaska Department of Fish and Game and looked it all over. It appeared that the big animals had fared pretty well in spite of that brutal winter, but I decided to do some serious survey work myself. Twelve hours of enjoyable flying over my favored hunting areas assured me that the coming fall hunts ought to be about normal, as I found good Dall sheep, moose, caribou and bear populations. On the last trip in the float plane I located a much higher than usual number of potential world class bull moose. That really surprised me. Not only did the severe winter not seem to have had an adverse effect on the big deer, but this looked like one of those years of extraordinarily good antler growth.

Our first guests in August were a man and his wife from the Steiermark region in Austria. Edmund and Johanna were a most delightful couple with a lot of hunting experience in Europe but this was their first trip to the Great Land. I give details of their two huge moose in another story titled, "Frau Eder and Me" which appears in *ALASKA HUNTING: Earthworms to Elephants*. But suffice it to say that they both took capital, world class bulls and marveled at the abundance of exotic mushrooms

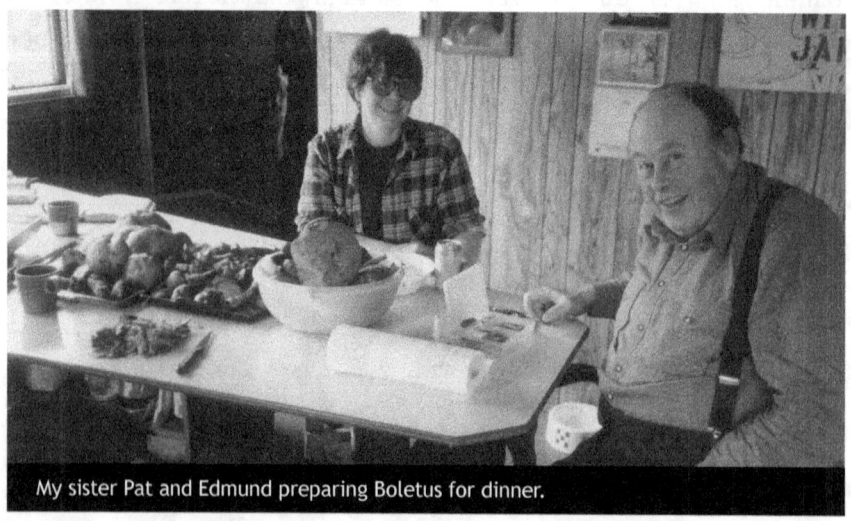

Cousin Steve Nason and Max with a huge Boletus

My sister Pat and Edmund preparing Boletus for dinner.

available for us to enjoy. Some of the Boletus fungi grow as large as a loaf of bread!

Following the Eders, I had my old friend Ulrich (Ulo) from West Germany who lives near the Elbe River on the border to East Germany along with three younger West Germans named Gunter, Christoph and Ulrich. Ulo had taken a fine moose, a good grizzly, several caribou, and a dandy Dall ram on previous hunts, so he was satisfied to have us concentrate on providing opportunities for his younger countrymen to hunt moose and sheep while he pursued another grizzly, caribou and photography.

On August 28, their hunt began the first morning when we spotted a band of three exceptionally good rams about five miles up Trail Creek valley. I had carefully glassed these rams earlier that season and knew they were all well over a full curl of maybe forty inches, with heavy bases. These three were all trophies at the top of their class. So, off we went with lunches in our packs and enthusiasm exuding from every pore. The big sheep crossed McKenzie pass and grazed up Big Baldy Knob which looked good for giving us an opportunity to get within decent range, but three hours into our trip, as we neared the summit, a heavy cloud cover moved in and obscured our vision. After sitting for ninety minutes with the chilling fog descending ever lower on the mountain I decided to break off this pursuit as I feared that if we buggered those old rams we would never get sight of them again that season. If, on the other hand, we didn't spook those old fellows, we might get a chance at them another day.

Our guests were in good spirits as we returned toward the lodge. When we stopped to take a drink from a cool mountain creek I sighted a band of approximately eight hundred caribou coming down Trail Creek toward us.

It happened to be Christoph's birthday, so Gunter and Christoph's brother, Ulrich, insisted that the birthday boy should be given the option to shoot first. We hunkered down in some brush near the mouth of Current Creek and waited for the impressive mass of tundra deer to come to us. When the moving biomass was 150 meters from us we watched as the biggest bulls bringing up the rear end of the herd came closer. Christoph shot well and acquired a big bull along with a scope cut eyebrow, otherwise known as "the Weatherby Award."

Christoph with his birthday bull.

Ulrich with his bull from the same bunch.

Gunter and his dandy, before coffee, bull.

Christoph's bull would place number two in the statewide competition for the year.

The moving mass of caribou were oblivious to the single rifle shot and our presence. They kept on with their southerly migratory movement and another "taker" loomed up. Ulrich decided to take one as well.

Christoph's special Weatherby award drew a lot of guffaws from the others, all of which he took with a hearty laugh and an extra toast to the miracle of his birth, his wonderful luck, and as many other things worthy of a toast as the trio could dream up. It was a happy first evening in camp.

On the second morning as coffee was being poured another big band of several hundred caribou came down the opposite side of Trail Creek. I hustled Gunter across the river and after only a thirty minute stalk Gunter secured his bull which measured up to be the number one caribou for the year in the statewide competition.

I sent one Assistant Guide, Loren, back up creek to glass for the big rams while I prepared the cub for a trip back to Kotzebue with Ulrich and a load of meat and antlers. We would unload, put the meat and antlers away, then jump in the float plane to try to locate a big moose and set up our camp nearby before dark.

Our timing was spot on and just before it was too dark to land we located two big bulls about three quarters of a mile from my favorite camping lake. We were too close to risk a fire so we ate a cold supper and quietly settled into our bags in the tent. Some home made German pear brandy assisted the sandman and we were soon sleeping.

As light began to grace the horizon I was up pouring coffee from the thermos. A quick bear claw pastry from the grocery supplies and we were on our way toward the location of the big bulls we had seen. We came onto five moose just a quarter of a mile from the tent. Their nocturnal meanderings had brought them right to us, probably because the big bulls had sensed the three cows which now helped compose the bunch. When we had light enough to distinguish their headgear I told Ulrich which was the best and he shot true, as is usually the case with German hunters. The big bull lurched forward and abruptly disappeared from view. The other moose seemed shellshocked and did not move until we were close.

As we searched for the fallen moose we found some splotches of blood, but no animal. After nearly a half hour of searching, I went back to the area Ulrich had stood when he fired and then walked to the area I had last seen the bull. Another fifty yards into the dense bush and I saw the dead moose. The mortally wounded critter had lurched into a depression and fallen head first into a muddy bog at the bottom. One had to be within a few feet of the carcass to see any sign of the big animal.

When at last I saw the targeted animal with the left antler buried in a wallow, only the right horn was visible. That was a first time experience for me.

The bull was a bit unhandy to butcher.

No decent photographs of the trophy could be taken until I had quartered and completely butchered the animal in the soft, muddy wallow, which in late August had not yet been anointed with moose urine and did not smell as bad as they do once bulls have peed into them. Once decapitated and fully exposed, the rack proved to be a world class wall hanger with wide palms and beautiful symmetry. Ulrich was beside himself at having taken such a capital trophy! I told him that I would make the eight short trips to get the meat to the plane if he wanted to relax at the lakeshore.

Before mid morning when I returned to the tent with the fifth load of meat Ulrich was bathing nude in the lake. He said he wanted to swim above the Arctic Circle and he appeared to be enjoying the chill water and crisp autumn air. A resident Tundra Swan group of two adults and three gray signets seemed not to mind sharing their lake However the birds stayed close to the opposite bank.

After loading the backstraps (all the meat from the rump to the base of the ears on each side) and tenderloins into the float compartments, I tied the rack to the float struts and soon had Ulrich and the camping gear loaded. After the ninety minute trip to town, I unloaded, fueled up and returned for the rest of the meat. We had secured a super moose with only

This rack was as appealing as any I have ever seen.

one night in the tent - and it was still a day away from the opener of Grizzly season on the first of September!

We dined on moose filet mignon with red wine in Kotzebue that evening and by mid morning the next day we were flying back to the lodge.

The previous day had been active for all in camp, but no big game was taken. Two wolves, a gray and a black, had been spotted which kept the hunters occupied for the entire day without producing an opportunity for anyone to shoot. Smaller bands of caribou were trickling down the drainage, but no great racks were spotted. They reported many ptarmigan in the tundra and a good many huge spawning Arctic Char in the creek.

September first dawned clear and chilly. Over the years I had sprained both my knees on several occasions but they got better on their own. However for reasons unknown to me both knees were bothering me a lot when bear season rolled around. I suppose it might have been due to the heavy loads I routinely packed. I had carried out the meat of three moose within the last two weeks.

We walk from the lodge on all hunts that we conduct in the valley. I headed toward the South Overlook - about four and a half air miles from the lodge along with my black labrador, Max, Gunter, Ullrich and Andy, an assistant. I detailed the events of that day in a story titled "The Rogue Sow", which is in my book -ALASKA BEARS: Stirred and Shaken but the short of it is, Gunter took a huge sow grizzly that rushed us and received the award for #2 Grizzly in the state competition. Max played a pivotal role in preventing the wounded, charging, bear from getting to me. After Uli had chewed me out for endangering his friend, Gunter told Uli to just shut up, then he told us that day was the most exciting and memorable in his entire life. I packed the bear skin back to the lodge and was surprised to notice that my knees seemed to be improving.

That same day Ulo, Christoph and Loren, my other assistant, scored on a boar grizzly just across the creek from the lodge.

On September second I took Gunter back to Kotzebue, transferred to the float plane and headed for the prime moose country. Moose were out and looking for love much more actively than just a few days before. We found several impressive bulls in heavy cover a few miles from where I had camped with Ulrich, so I landed and set up camp on the shore of one of my favorite lakes.

This time a light, but steady wind and sufficient distance from the animals allowed us to enjoy a nice little fire with grilled game meat and stick bread flavored with butter and garlic. Like most Germans, Gunter savored the wilderness, its smells, the abundant variety of flowers and berries, and most of all, the total absence of man-made noises. A pair of Arctic Loons serenaded us, followed by the distant, lonesome howl of a wolf. My guest and I soaked up the essence of Alaska at its best.

Shortly before dawn as I was preparing a light breakfast the mournful bawl of a cow moose rolled across the lake. The bulls would have heard it too, so we grabbed our packs and rifles and started off toward the sound.

Large black spruce and a few cottonwoods ringed the lake. Adjacent to the bigger timber grew dense stands of young birch and willows. Moose had browsed the succulent young tops off uniformly as though trimmed by a conscientious gardener, but in many areas the tops were well above our heads, restricting our visibility and making our passage a noisy one.

Multiple Species Hunts after a TOUGH WINTER

Max, grinning with Gunter and the rogue Grizzly.

An ideal campsite in great moose country. Note aircraft in background.

A beautiful, windless evening.

After twenty minutes of slow travel the cow bawled again confirming that we were on the right course to approach her location.

As we crept through the jungle I heard the unmistakable sound of moose antlers scraping brush. We froze in mid step. Our ears told us that several big animals were moving just in front of us, but beyond our limited field of vision. Gunter whispered to me that he liked the smell of the Hudson Bay tea we crushed as we walked over it. I nodded in agreement and motioned "quiet."

We glimpsed the massive brown forms of several moose as they maneuvered through the tangle toward the solicitous cow, but we never could confirm a big rack. By noon after traveling for only about a mile, we had reached a small ridge overlooking a broad valley with large open treeless spaces. It was an ideal place to sit and watch as we had our lunch.

The heat of the day led to our decision to take a short nap. The moose were likely doing the same thing at that time. An early frost had turned the leaves to resplendent reds, yellows and orange and had suppressed the ubiquitous mosquitos and white sox, so our naps were not interrupted by insects. Our dry aromatic tundra mattress was as comfortable as any feather bed.

Gunter awoke before I did and was sitting nearby taking in the grandeur of the country when I was jolted awake by the grunt of a bull moose. The animal was not far away and the noise came from back in the direction of our camp. I sat up and strained to hear more. After what seemed like half of forever I heard the tell-tale hollow sounds of an antler palm as it pushed aside vegetation.

We got to our feet and slipped into our pack boards, ready to respond to any opportunity. Sounds indicated the moose was walking slowly toward our position. A birch sapling moved as the bull stepped into view only to disappear before we could react. The antlers were huge with a blizzard of points and had a spread that I estimated to be in the seventy inch range. Before Gunter had a shot the giant melted into the brush and we lost sight of him.

Gunter's jaw dropped open and his eyes seemed as big as Elton John's sunglasses. I motioned for him to hold still. We could faintly hear the giant bull as he quartered away toward the lake.

My elation at finding such an outstanding bull was tempered by the difficulty of the situation. The thick brush prevented a clear shot. If wounded, this animal would be difficult to locate and if dropped in his tracks, packing the meat through such a place would amplify the danger of a close, unexpected encounter with a bear. But we both were struck by a powerful adrenalin rush. I raked the butt of my rifle up and down a few strokes on a bush, simulating the sound of an antler. This sometimes effective technique drew no response from the bull.

After a full ten minutes with no more sight or sound of the antlered giant I whispered to Gunter that we would follow along slowly, making our best effort to be quiet, mentioning my Dad's admonition to hunt big game as if it had a gun and was hunting you! Gunter nodded in agreement. We walked over several large piles of bear droppings.

Our route took us to a small hill within sight of the camp lake, so we proceeded ever so slowly along the crest of the hill, with long pauses to listen for our quarry. The ground was heavily pockmarked with hoof prints and well sprinkled with moose droppings - ranging from the loose plops of diarrhetic spring offal to the fresh, solid, "Alaska pecan" nuggets of summer, indicating that a sizable population of the big deer had used this area for several months. I doubted that the animals would vacate this prime pasture until heavy snows or wolves forced them out.

We agreed that we should be patient in our attempts to relocate the big bull.

As shadows grew longer and a chill developed I realized that it would soon be dark and it was time to head for camp. We had spent several hours of tense stalking since briefly glimpsing the bull. We had not walked very far, but I felt worn out. The tension had been heavy all day.

Time truly does fly when you're having fun.

We arrived at the tent just at dark. This time I felt it prudent to make no fire. Knowing that any number of moose, including the giant we had briefly glimpsed, may be close, we continued our conversations in low whispers. After a glass of red wine from a bladder flask, along with dried salmon and caribou meat, we settled into our sleeping bags. Sleep came slowly to me, then after midnight I awoke to the sound of a loud splash. I sat upright before my brain was fully engaged and I realized that a beaver had cruised in close, seen the float plane, became alarmed and slapped the lake surface with its tail. Gunter was up too, so I explained the noise to him. He commented on how wonderful it was to be disturbed in his sleep by a wild beaver and not a train whistle or an automobile horn.

I liked this guy and his attitude even more, the more time I spent with him.

After the beaver incident sleep was elusive for me and when it did come, it was shallow. Well before sunup we were ready to go after a cold cup of instant juice and a pastry. It was too dim to see well, so having heard nothing, I decided to remain near the tent until we had decent light. Full daylight revealed nothing to move us, but the memory of the giant moose lingered, urging action of some sort. Then I caught a fleeting glimpse of a moose paddle on the small hill where we had last followed behind the big one. I alerted Gunter and studied the area with my binoculars. Minutes passed with nothing happening. As the sun rose, more dark shadows materialized, but none moved. Then again I saw the light colored forward side of a moose paddle as the bull moved through the dense cover. The bull was slowly walking, turning his head from side to side, displaying his rack to intimidate other bulls and impress cows. This animal was coming off the ridge and toward our lake, but was it the giant?

Gunter wanted to go after the bull, but I figured we should remain where we were with better visibility from the tent site across the lake from the moose. We needed to positively identify the bull we wanted before committing ourselves to the thicket.

A cow bawled way off behind us. I hoped the moose's auditory radar had received her call. If so, it might draw him toward us. I imagined the bulls semaphore-like ears rotating to pick up the cow's bawl.

A few hardy mosquito and whitesox survivors of the early frost homed in on us and soon were joined by squadrons of their kin. Avoiding any unnecessary noise, we just quietly smashed the little bloodsuckers, rather than slap them.

Half of forever can be a long, long time to stand waiting and that seemed to be what we were enduring when a huge moose stepped out of the denser cover into a more open part of the hillside. If it wasn't the same great beast we glimpsed the day before, but it was a dandy and a taker for sure. Still we waited.

Moose don't see all that well, but he stood still, surveying the area, slowly moving his head to display his antlers, working his ears forward and back, listening. Moose of both sexes do seem to be able to detect opponents' antlers. We didn't move or twitch. I wished that I had a shed moose horn or a bleached white scapula to hold up. If so, I think I could have brought him right in. I had forgotten my caribou scapula back at the lodge in the pack I used on the bear hunt.

A "mulligan moose" - a one or two year old bull - stepped out of the thicket between us and the big one. Then the big fellow of the previous day slowly walked toward the youngster, displaying his super sized rack. It was him! Unmistakably! Believing the great one's attention would be on this wannabe competitor, we retreated to the spruce trees behind us, then began to circle the lake to reduce the distance to the animals.

At the edge of the timber nearest the moose we watched the two bulls approach each other. At twenty feet the young bull suddenly became a believer, wheeled, and turned back toward us at a full gallop with the big bull following.

The 72 inch bull as he fell.

Gunter was ready and squeezed his trigger when the big moose was only sixty yards away. The impact of the 8mm bullet caused the bull to stop initially, but the stricken moose abruptly wheeled around and ran back up the hill. I told Gunter not to shoot him in the butt. The wounded moose was soon out of sight but I had noted a dead spruce near where we last saw him and we rapidly made for that landmark. As we neared the snag the bull struggled to stand up, then went down in front as his forelegs failed. I told Gunter to put a shot in the neck. The great body collapsed with all four feet stiffly extended straight out.

Gunter was speechless again. What a moose!

Patience is the hunter they say, and on this hunt that philosophy was again confirmed. My video camera recorded the shooting and Gunter's open mouth reaction which would prove to be a highlight of the annual video production. After recovering from the second great adrenalin rush in as many days, we made the photos and began butchering the huge beast. Gunter insisted on helping pack the meat. We had to go uphill a short way, but most of the trip was descending the gentle slope through the birch and

Gunter packing out his trophy.

willows to the camp. Each leg of the four trips we made took about twenty-five minutes. It was not a bad pack at all, but I was seeing a lot of bear poop!

Gunter asked to be left at the lake as I flew the first load to town, but I told him I needed his help with unloading the meat, so he agreed to go with me. I always took the guest out in the first load to avoid any possible problems due to bears, a delay in the second trip, and so forth. He cut one last sprig of aromatic Hudson Bay tea to stick in his hat and reluctantly climbed into the back seat of the cub.

I got my guest back to Kotzebue with the trophy and some meat on the first trip. After refueling the plane I returned to our campsite and loaded the rest of the meat in the cub for the second trip to town. This bull had a huge body as well as a big rack. The floats were completely submerged up to the aft spreader bar as I taxied to make use of the full length of the lake, but the lake was plenty long enough and the light wind was favorable, allowing me to lift off with water to spare.

Once landed and unloaded in Kotzebue I refueled and got back to the shack in time to grill up some bacon wrapped tenderloins for our meal of moose filet mignon.

The tape measured a seventy-two inch spread and this rack won Gunter the third place trophy for moose in 1989.

Back at the lodge by noon the next day I was pleased to learn that Ulo had taken a good caribou and enough Willow Ptarmigan to feed all eight of us a big meal and stock the lunches for the next day. Teresa was at the skillet for a long time. Dozens of caribou continued to drift down the valley each day. Dall sheep on the mountains to the east and west were seen every day, but the big trio we lost on the first day had not showed themselves since that first day when we lost them in the fog.

The next day we set out looking for rams. Andy took Christoph to Current Creek and I took Gunter to the Big Cirque basin on the east side. Ulrich decided to stay in camp to read, though we all encouraged him to hunt.

Ulo preferred to do some filming of fish and whatever else he could find, so I had Loren accompany him.

At the head of Big Cirque I glassed two rams lying on a promontory. They were both over a curl so we took the only approach available to us - straight up the creek bottom, often in sight of the sheep. Before crossing open places I would glass the rams, then when the sheep were not looking our way, we would slowly move to the next cover.

So it went for three hours. When we were six hundred yards directly below the rams, and out of their sight, we quickly ascended the last and steepest slope on our hands and knees. I told Gunter that I expected we would top out about two hundred yards from the rams and then determine which was the better one to shoot.

But as we eased over the top the rams were not there! So we waited. Time seemed to drag along. Sweat ran into my eyes and as I wiped them, I caught sight of a small patch of white. One of the rams began to come into view as he fed out of a small gully between us and the high promontory. We were less than one hundred yards from the sheep, but below them! I motioned to Gunter to load his chamber, be quiet and wait. Before the first ram was in full view the head of the other appeared. I motioned to Gunter to take

Gunter, pleased with his ram.

the second ram as soon as he was ready. A gentle waving of my hand indicated that he should not be in a hurry. I thought I heard Gunter's heart beating - or maybe it was my own. He appeared tense and anxious, as I certainly was. The second ram - the one we wanted - walked out of sight, heightening the tension. In a few minutes the larger ram reappeared and offered an ideal broadside shot. Without hesitation, Gunter fired, hitting the ram just behind the front shoulders and sending him tumbling down the slope toward us.

Camera problems visited both of us that afternoon, but a photograph back in the lodge yard helped preserve the memory.

"I tell you my friend, all the animals seem to come to you when you are ready to shoot. Maybe they want to take you up on an all expense paid trip to your trophy room, in Germany" I told him.

"Yah, especially the grizzly, Jake!"

It was a fine ten year old ram of more than a full curl with the right horn broomed off about an inch. So this was Gunter's fourth big game animal in a bit less than a full week of hunting.

Each animal had come toward him as he shot. The grizzly had come toward him in a rush. He had the #1 Caribou, the #2 Grizzly and the #3 Moose and a dandy Dall Ram and he told me long before the last day, that it had been the best trip of his life.

Once again Gunter insisted on helping with packing out the meat and trophy. As we walked out of the basin he took time to smell the flowers, enjoy the pure cold mountain water and savor the several types of berries.

Christoph with his super ram.

Christoph and Andy had returned to the lodge ahead of us and they had found one of the three big sheep we had seen on day one. It was alone and feeding high on the western slope of Current Creek. They were able to approach to within less than one hundred yards and the ram dropped in its tracks after one shot. This magnificent ram measured over forty inches in length and had large bases. It ranked number one in the statewide competition.

Fresh blueberry pie topped off a superb meal of moose and caribou steaks. The sheep tenderloins would go great with eggs in the morning.

After breakfast I drained ten gallons of gas (sixty pounds) from the cub and loaded as much meat as I dared before taking Christoph back to town.

Things went as normal and we flew out late in the afternoon to the productive moose range.

Weather continued to be good. I had put only an extra ten gallons of gas in the belly tank giving us a total of over six hours of flying time when we lifted off Honey Bucket lake in Kotzebue. We flew the usual ninety minutes to the area that had been so good all season and began to see bulls demonstrating pre-rut behavior immediately. We had a full two hours before dark and so I flew throughout the foothills area looking at more than fifty mature bulls. The horny beasts were not at all intimidated by the aircraft. Some bulls rushed toward the sound of the engine and some that I inadvertently flew directly over reared up to strike at us with their hooves, though we were three to six hundred feet above them.

The bulls were hot and spoiling for a fight, or a lover.

I noticed a lone cow running across an open area. Less than fifty yards behind her came a large grizzly at a lope. The cow appeared to be tired when she came to a small lake. Without hesitation she went in with a splash and began swimming for the opposite shore. The bear paused at the edge of the water, apparently analyzing the situation before turning to run along the margin of the lake to intercept the moose. As the cow came to within thirty yards of the far shore she saw the bear, stopped and began treading water when she realized the bear would meet her if she stepped out. Had there been more cover for the grizzly the moose would likely have stepped out of the water into the claws and teeth of the big bear.

I pulled down full flaps and slowly circled the lake as we watched the scenario unfold. The bear swung his head from side to side, frustrated, obviously expecting to be dining on that moose for the next week or so.

The moose looked young and confused, but turned back to the middle of the lake and rested as she tried to organize her strategy for her next move. We made several circles before the bear plunged into the lake, turning the moose back the way she had come. The grizzly's move was only a feint, as he quickly returned to the shore and ran hard once again to meet the moose. We had our own hunting to do, so had to depart leaving the two great beasts to their individual fates. Two days later I flew by the lake and found the bear embracing the pile of tundra he had heaped upon the moose carcass. We had witnessed the beginning of a triumph of intelligence and strength over mere biomass. Poor moose.

As was often the case, I did not locate a specific bull to pursue, but I landed the plane on a lake with good visibility, a comfortable camping spot and several adult moose of both sexes within a mile or less. We would wait to see what developed the next day. With such an abundance of moose in the area, this was the most reasonable strategy.

Circumstances permitted a camp fire followed by foil baked potatoes, grilled sheep meat and freshly picked blue berries. We laid back on the soft tundra and reflected on how lucky we were to be blessed with this beautiful evening in such a miraculous sector of untainted wild land.

First there was a single distant call, then two yelps. The sounds increased until a gentle chorus of many geese could be heard as strings of southward bound birds passed overhead and faded away over the mountains into the twilight.

One bird had become separated from the great flocks and winged over us at low level. I gave my best "uuuhh ahhhh" voice call and the lonesome young White Front goose banked, turned back to our lake and landed just in front of the airplane, providing us with one of my favorite scenes - that of a goose setting its wings and dropping its feet for a water landing. Once on the water the juvenile goose glanced about nervously, extending its neck to right and left as it studied its surroundings. Not comfortable with the strange machine nearby, it quickly turned, splashed away over the surface, got airborne and headed off to the south.

As the last light of the day faded, a small flock of Pintail ducks landed across the lake and chuckled as they settled in for the night. Christoph and I quietly crawled into our bags, avoiding noise that might alarm our water fowl cohabitants. The company of the ducks added to our feeling of contentment. It was a beautiful, peaceful evening.

The friendly sky of the preceding evening had morphed into a sullen overcast before we left our bags the next morning. My assessment of the weather brought to mind the intense storm that had thrashed Frau Eder and I just two weeks before. I went to the plane and was able to hear the weather report as given on the NDB (non-directional beacon) in Kotzebue. It mentioned another weakening typhoon coming our way from the South Pacific. I lifted the tail of the cub to seat the heels of the floats a little further up on the beach and tightened the securing lines before we walked toward a better position to visually dissect the area with our binoculars.

Before noon we had identified seven moose, of which two were large bulls, but they were too distant to judge conclusively. Before mid afternoon we were being pelted with large raindrops driven by a gale force wind. One squall after another visited us with occasional brief breaks in the

In the fog in the back country.

overcast and a slackening of the wind, allowing the sun's energy to produce a mist rising from the dampened tundra. The surreal landscape invited photographic activity, so we both exposed some film.

Clearly we were not going to find a trophy moose without covering more ground so we set off in the direction of what appeared to be the better of the two bulls. After a half mile of travel we came to a narrow stream trenching its way through the tundra. The water was dark, which usually indicates a depth above our hip boots, so we skirted it until we came to a sharp bend with opposing banks close enough to permit a fit man to clear it with a running jump. I backed off and charged the ditch clutching my rifle and swinging it ahead of me as I leaped. Part of the bank gave way as I landed but my momentum carried me clear of the water. Christoph followed and we were once again headed directly for the big bull.

We came to an elongated swale which was not visible from our previous vantage point and in it were several moose which we had not seen earlier. Three large bulls were standing nose to nose, apparently deliberating which had the greatest qualifications to be suitor to the nearby cows. Brief periods of sunshine produced diamond-like sparkles off the water in the palms of their antlers.

Christoph is pleased with his trophy.

The aft view of antlered game always makes their headgear look its best and Christoph wanted to shoot the bull with its tail toward us. I cautioned him to wait and watch. A slight breeze came from them to us and all the animals seemed oblivious to our presence, so there was no need to be in a hurry. I glassed the area for yet another bull, but found no more. As the big fellows slowly changed their positions, it became evident which had the greatest antlers and I told Christoph he could go ahead and shoot.

The first round impacted the bull just behind the shoulder and he hunched up, standing in place. I told Christoph to "shoot him again." The second round dropped the bull as if it had been brain shot. One of the competitors nosed the fallen monarch and snorted a visible puff of steam. The standing bulls turned and walked slowly toward the cows.

The fallen bull was a dandy and when back in town we measured it at over sixty-seven inches in width with great palms and fourteen points on each side. We began to butcher the downed bull with an audience of several live moose until after a half hour they began to drift away. I cut the four quarters off quickly, leaving the skin on to shed rain and better protect the meat. The skin would be removed before taking the meat to town. We worked rapidly and in less than an hour we had the job done.

As we had one and a half to two miles of difficult terrane and the deep creek between us and the camp lake I decided to take a look over the next small ridge before starting back with the first loads of meat.

On the far side of our swale was another similar, but larger depression with a lake suitable for the cub with light loads. It took about fifteen minutes to pack a big load from the kill site to that lake. After we packed the meat to the small lake I could ferry two plane loads of meat to camp, thereby exchanging a short back packing transport of the meat for the long arduous route that brought us there.

Luck was on our side, again.

Our trip back to camp with only tenderloins and heart took little over an hour, putting us at the tent a half hour after dark in a slight breeze and slow drizzle. It had been another very good day, overall.

It was still raining in the morning. I flew Christoph to the short lake and we began packing the four loads apiece from the kill site. After the third load, my guest suggested that I make the first meat trip back to the camp with the airplane, while he brought out the last load of meat and the head. It was a capital idea, with which I agreed. Once I had the last load of meat and the head ready to shuttle back to the camping site, Christoph offered that I could take the first load to town while he hiked back to camp, then he could pack up the tent and other aspects of camp, while I was making the first meat run to Kotzebue. But I insisted that I get him to camp where we could take down the tent and he would accompany me to town on the first trip. As good as most of my guests were, I was not comfortable with leaving them alone so far from help. So I did my usual thing, taking Christoph, the camping gear, the head, tenderloins and back straps to town. I returned for the bulk of the meat and landed with the last load in Kotzebue just after dark. If it's working -- don't fix it, I've always figured.

I did not take Christoph back to the lodge as his group was scheduled to come out the next day. He was content to stay in town trimming meat off of the skulls for eventual European mounts.

So, after twelve days of hunting, our three guests from West Germany had taken three great moose, two exceptional Dall rams, three fine caribou and a huge grizzly bear. Ulo had taken a grizzly and a caribou during that same period. Dozens of ptarmigan were shot and put to the skillet as well.

Multiple Species Hunts after a TOUGH WINTER

Gunter with his #1 Caribou, #2 Grizzly, #3 Moose and a dandy Dall Ram.

Christoph and Gunter with the fine collection our three guests harvested.

For 1989 they earned #1 Dall Ram, #1 and #2 Caribou, #2 Grizzly and #3 Moose. That's one of the most successful hunts I know of for high quality animals, as well as truly appreciative guests. Christoph told me that German taxidermist, Wolfgang Shenk, had reported it to be the best collection that he had seen from Alaska since the Kunert's in 1987.

And we had more guests that season. On the last hunt of the year the wolves which had been working Trail Creek valley had so terrorized the other big game that, after several instances of seeing bull moose running in front of cows and the bands of southward migrating caribou smoking through the country without pause to feed, I decided to base our last two hunters, both of whom were primarily interested in moose, out of Kotzebue, using the float plane and tent camps.

Alan with his two caribou and bull moose.

The first, Allan, took a fine moose with his rifle in the area I had been hunting all fall and collected two bull caribou from a tent camp I put in with the float plane south of the lodge, on a lake that had become known as "Jake's Lake."

The other hunter, Lloyd, anchored a big bull with his bow at less than twenty yards.

Lloyd with his bow killed bull.

After a record setting severe winter we had enjoyed a record setting hunting season … and I had not needed to fly a single piece of ice to Trail Creek to keep our food fresh and our drinks cold.

For months I had been worried that the severe winter would decimate the big game populations only to experience as good a season as I had ever seen, with antler development in moose and caribou as good as it gets.

So many variables come into play in nature.

A Double on Grizzlies

The 2011 Fall Season began in December 2009 with a phone call from a man in Louisiana. He came across as a typical, courteous southern gentleman. He wanted to come with his son and a nephew to hunt every big game specie we had, so I made applications for each man for grizzly, Dall ram and moose, but none were drawn for a permit. Caribou, Wolves and Wolverine could be hunted without a drawn permit. This is the first time so many applications for hunters in a single group of mine failed to be awarded even one permit.

But this gentleman was persistent and he asked that I make applications again for the 2011 season. The drawing results were much different this time with all three men being drawn for a grizzly permit, the elder man receiving a Dall ram permit and a moose permit.

Drawings are a real frustration to guides, as well as would be hunters, but in an ever more crowded world, drawings offer the most objective way of allocating hunting permits.

Ron, my assistant guide, had asked to bring his lady friend, Vicki and her son Sean up in late August before the Louisiana group arrived. This provided us a week of preparation for the booked hunters and a nice introduction to the Arctic for Sean.

On day two, we observed two large grizzlies in a fight across the main river. I got a little of the action on my video, but it was from long range. The great beasts would lower their heads, swinging noticeably until they rushed at each other. At times they seemed to embrace as do boxers in a clench, then they would break, stand off and go at it again. One of their clashes lasted for nearly half an hour. Neither bruin showed sign of injury from the fights. I did not see any fur fly.

We saw the pair of bears several times during the last week of August. The darker one was the slightly larger of the two. These bears were not familiar to me. I believe they recently moved onto Trail Creek from the surrounding country.

We all enjoyed some snowshoe rabbit hunting and the day of Vicki and Sean's departure, Ron took them across the river where Sean harvested a young bull caribou. That was another eleventh hour caribou.

Conditions were about what I had come to expect for the area in late August and early September. Our Dipwater Creek was flowing nicely and the tundra was in its normally damp condition. Berries of all types were plentiful, which was a dramatic contrast to the previous summer.

On August 31, the first hunting day with the Louisiana group, I took the elder man, Bob, to look for a ram in Current Creek, while Ron took Will and Jeb into West Bowl to check out some caribou. About a half mile into the Current Creek valley I glassed a ram that showed exceptionally heavy horn bases with the curl so deep it was visible well below its jaw line. This was a very impressive ram. Such depth to the curl indicated each horn would measure over thirty-eight inches, but the horns were not broomed and each showed a bit less than a full curl. The regulations read that a legal ram must be full curl, broomed, or a minimum of eight years of age. The age of a ram is often argued between seasoned biologists and I had never taken a ram with less than a full curl or broomed horns. I was certain this ram must be eight years of age or older, but depending on the count of annular rings could be a trap. We admired that fine ram for nearly an hour with binoculars before returning to the main valley.

Bob and I got to the lodge before the others, so I began preparing a spaghetti dinner. About the time to boil the pasta, the trio showed up heavily laden with caribou meat and antlers. They had encountered a band of about fifty animals on a high bench across the river from the lodge from which Jeb and Will each took a bull. Ron dragged the carcasses to the edge of the bench to make the gut piles easily visible from the lodge.

These were neither old nor large caribou, but Ron and I had discussed the situation. With us having three guests with grizzly permits, the caribou limit of five animals per hunter, and the always unsure availability of caribou, we needed to harvest some handy ones to not only fill the first

A Double on Grizzlies

Will and Jeb with Jeb's first caribou.

Will's smile is as colorful as the countryside.

tags and provide camp meat, but we might benefit from the presence of gut piles attracting grizzly bears, wolves and/or wolverine.

For breakfast on September 1, the opening day of grizzly season, we had caribou tenderloins, bacon, eggs and coffee. As I began to gather up the dishes I noticed a strange dark shadow on one of the gut piles. Before I could put the tripod mounted spotting scope on it, I saw there were large objects on both gut piles. The quarrelsome pair of grizzlies had found the site of the previous day's kills. Excitement filled the room!

Normally it takes a large grizzly about eight days to consume an entire moose and I reckoned the bears would be on the gut piles throughout most of the day, but not much longer. We quickly plastered together some sandwiches, bagged some cookies and each man grabbed an apple. We were soon off toward the feeding grizzlies.

There was little wind and the infrequent zephyrs that I detected were coming from down creek, so we hiked for the bench end downwind from the bears. We were able to keep the kill site in view most of the trip, but when we reached the base of the steep mountain we could no longer see the area.

Twenty yards below the edge of the bench I told the three shooters to "put one up the spout" and engage the safety. I had my video camera at the ready and Ron chambered a round. We proceeded the final distance ever so slowly until I located the dark, larger bear, then the other one. The dark one was lying atop his claimed gut pile with his head down, but pointed in our direction. The lighter colored grizzly had its back to us as it fussed with its trove of culinary treasure.

Jeb was to be the first shooter. I nodded to him and Will to take aim and fire when ready. This was off-hand shooting at sixty yards for Jeb and about eighty yards for Will.

The two men fired almost simultaneously. Jeb's bear simply shuddered and remained in place, dead with its spine crushed just behind the head, but Will's beast twisted around and bit at the area just behind its left shoulder. I hollered at Will to keep shooting until the bear was down. Two more shots found their mark as the bear tried to climb up the hill and away from us. A fourth round broke its back just forward of the pelvis and the bear came tumbling down the hill toward our group of five men. It raised up on its front legs just as Will squeezed again and the bear was down and done.

A Double on Grizzlies

Jeb's grizzly placed third in the 2011 statewide competition.

Will's boar was twelve years of age and unmarked.

This boar was fifteen years of age and a rough looking customer, but he went down easily. Suddenly the valley was quiet.

A great wave of relief rolled through the group. I had never before approached even a single bear with so many people. Upon quick inspection I saw that both bears were mature males. This is the first time I had ever taken part in harvesting two boars in such close proximity to each other.

It's curious, and extremely unusual, that two mature boars would tolerate each other's presence as these two had done. These bears were not siblings as there was a three year difference in their ages. Normally the larger bear would have injured, killed, or run off the younger boar. I guess this may be an example of how it's not so important how big the dog in a fight is, but how much fight is in the dog ... or grizzly.

Ours was an exhilarated and happy group.

We took our time skinning and with so many able people to help pack, we took the hinds from both bears. Yes, they had been feeding on meat, but it was likely the first meat they had eaten in months and it would not have had time to taint the meat. This bear meat was all prime and the hinds were consumed by us and friends in Kotzebue. Oddly enough, bears have very small back straps, so we do not save them.

Ron whipped up a big supper of caribou back straps, baked potatoes and a huge salad with a platter of fresh baked brownies for dessert.

The next morning our guests rose a bit later than usual. Ron and I had already downed a pot of coffee. The day was sunny and warm with little wind. I suggested Ron and I should closely flesh both bear hides, then we'd salt them and put them on the frames to dry. More than a week would pass before the hides could be placed in a freezer.

Our guests had expressed interest in fishing so we sent them down the creek, carrying their rifles, of course. They still had more caribou to harvest, a bear for Bob, and It would be nice for them to add some wolf hides to their bag - most important - we never go anywhere without a protective firearm to use if necessary against grizzlies.

As Ron and I sat in the sunshine outside the sauna building we were visited - and entertained - by a pair of Northern Shrikes. These so-called "butcher birds" *(Lanius borealis)* are the only carnivorous song birds that I am aware of in northwest Arctic Alaska. We had seen this pair hover in

A Double on Grizzlies

Jeb and Will figured it doesn't get much better than that!

Bob is profoundly proud of his son Will and his nephew, Jeb.

front of the windows of the lodge. Such was a common summer observation, but I had never before noticed a shrike hovering near me while I was outside. The pair of birds landed and perched on a willow branch and they seemed to emit several different calls. This was the first time I had ever heard one sing. The birds' actions seemed to make time fly for us as we removed the last of the fat from the bear skins. I did not see either bird show interest in any of the fat scraps we flung their way. Jays and Robins would have been fighting to get at the fat.

In my distracted state of euphoria over the double bear kills, I completely forgot that none of our guests had fishing licenses. It came to me when I saw them walking up the runway on their return. They had each caught and released Arctic Char and Grayling, but even "catch and release" required a license. I quickly did the paperwork for each man.

The next day was spent glassing the many passing caribou, looking for outstanding racks, but finding only mediocre headgear. About five o'clock we were visited by three small planes, each was an SQ2 - souped-up versions of a Super Cub or perhaps a Fieseler Storch from World War II. These planes had movable slots on the leading edges of the wings, similar to a Heliocourier. They were much more roomy than a cub and had the option to assist take-off with nitrous oxide. I was very impressed.

I invited our drop-in guests to the lodge for coffee and smoked salmon. One of the fellows expressed interest in buying the property and guide business. As we visited a band of three dozen caribou came down the moguls from East Bowl Creek. Timing could not have been better on that. I took Will and rushed over to give him an opportunity. He took the best caribou for the season so far, at less than eighty yards.

Ron returned with Bob and Jeb just as our surprise guests were departing.

They had glassed several sheep and two single grizzlies, but shot nothing.

We enjoyed a fine supper of caribou back straps, baked potato and salad followed by one of Ron's chocolate cakes.

Right after supper, Jeb and Will took the .22 and a shotgun and went looking for snowshoe hare and ptarmigan. They were soon back with a couple hares each which would make a fine meal for our group of five men.

Bob had an oil services company to manage and he brought his own satellite telephone to allow him to frequently check on things. He mentioned that one of his key men was ill and that might require that he return prior to the end of his booked hunting period. Will and Jeb expressed their hopes that an early departure would not be necessary.

A Double on Grizzlies

Will's bull shows some nice palmation on both antlers.

Not bad, for a yard harvest.

Bob's bull went down hard.

Jeb's bull was anchored with one shot.

The next morning was cold and windy. Bob was on his telephone early and announced that his key man had died and he needed to return to Louisiana as soon as possible. I gave him the charter pilot's phone number and he scheduled a trip for noon. It would require another charter to get the meat and hides out, but at least Bob could get to Kotzebue and arrange the flights back home. Bob had no more than ended his call when Ron hollered that there were caribou on the runway.

As near as I could count there were between seventy and a hundred caribou coming right up the creek from just below the runway. Bob had yet to shoot anything, so he would be the first to select a bull. Jeb had an unfilled tag in his pocket.

All five of us sneaked down through the willows until we were within three hundred yards of the nearest decent bulls. It did not look like we would be able to get closer. There were no outstanding bulls in the bunch.

We had some hustling to do to get the animals cut up and back to the lodge, but here, within my pattered eighty acres, we could use the Honda and trailer. As we were butchering the animals, Bob glassed some Dall sheep up in the big cirque basin of East Bowl Creek. He had an unfilled sheep tag and asked Ron or me to go to the lodge to scrutinize the animal with the spotting scope. My knife was already bloody, so Ron volunteered and I stayed with the butchery.

In a few minutes Ron was back. He said the animal was a ram, looked legal, and Bob wanted to try to get it. I went back to the lodge and reminded Bob that he had a charter coming in three hours which should be cancelled if he was going for the sheep. The pilot would not sit and wait for passengers. I went back to the caribou with the Honda and trailer. I assumed Bob made a call to cancel. Jeb volunteered to go with Bob, so Will and I got the fresh meat to the lodge and hung on the meat racks.

Right at twelve o'clock noon the chartered Cessna 206 landed. The pilot was in a hurry and asked where the passengers were. He had to interrupt his schedule to make this special trip. Apparently Bob had not called to cancel. I told the pilot that I guaranteed the trip would be paid in full and thanked him for his effort. We would call him when the group was next ready to depart.

But Old Murphy got into the act that afternoon. Steady strings with several hundred caribou came down the valley and right through the bog adjacent to the lodge - within easy shooting range of the lodge windows. I counted a dozen fine trophy racks, but Bob, with his unfilled tag, was not available and Will already had two bulls. It was frustrating to watch these magnificent bulls stroll past us, unconcerned. A few years earlier with a limit of five caribou for non-residents, I'm sure Will would have taken a dandy which would have placed in the annual "Big Three" competition.

About an hour before dark I spotted the trio coming off the east moguls and it looked like they were burdened with meat and a sheep cape, but there was a lightness to their steps. They obviously were pleased.

Jeb and his uncle Bob on a cold, windy hillside with the ram.

They went directly to the open hillside that held the lone ram, but they were unable to get above it. They glassed the beast and Ron deliberated for more than half an hour before he gave the okay to shoot. But shooting a questionable ram from below is always risky. The curl always looks more complete from below.

As soon as Ron and I were alone I told him to peel the cape off that head as soon as possible. We had to do a careful analysis of the annular rings. I was more than a little nervous that it may not show eight years of age. We would have to check it in, with the local biologist, no matter what its age. This was not the same ram Bob and I glassed on day one.

Careful counting revealed seven or eight annular rings. This put the age of the ram at eight or nine years. I breathed a sigh of relief.

Unfortunately the long strings of caribou had passed by the lodge hours before Bob returned, but nevertheless it had been a good day.

In his excitement to get up the mountain to pursue the ram, Bob had forgotten to cancel the charter for which he apologized to the pilot. The Cessna was booked to arrive at the lodge by ten the next morning.

What a day this had been! Everyone slept well that night.

Before I went to bed that evening I was satisfied that the ram was legal.

Will, Bob and Jeb with their smiles and trophies.

The charter came in on time and went out loaded with two guests, hides and several hundred pounds of meat. I took Will in the cub with the remainder of the meat.

I took Bob's sheep horns to the local Alaska Department of Fish and Game office. The biologist was out, so a young female employee came to measure and seal the sheep horns. This young woman was inexperienced and I anticipated questions with the less than full curl trophy. I asked for a protection officer and one came to seal the horns. I knew this fellow, who was a good man and knew his business. When he entered the room and first saw the horns he looked at me, twisted his head a bit and shot a questioning look my way.

"Yeah, I know it's not a full curl, Eric, but thankfully the annular rings show it's likely a nine year old," I offered. "Personally I would not have allowed the hunter to harvest this ram, but Ron and the shooter were positioned below the ram and convinced themselves that it was a full curl."

When the game warden counted the rings he came up with only seven for sure, with possibly an eighth ring.

"Okay, so we accept only the seven most distinct rings. That would be enough," I told him.

The warden gave me another questioning glance.

I drew a line on a piece of paper and put seven hash marks on it. Then I counted the spaces between the hash marks and there were eight. With the other possible ring, the sheep would have been nine years old, but it was at least eight years of age and that made it legal.

The protection officer agreed and the ram horns were sealed.

The hunters and I divvied up the meat. They had become aware of how tasty caribou meat can be and expressed their desire to take more than half, but I held firm, so Ron and I would have some for our tables.

The following morning the Louisiana trio boarded the jet and headed home. Since they left early, I had a day to wait for the next hunters to arrive, so I busied myself with paperwork and cleaning up the shack.

On September 10 the first hunter and I departed for the lodge. This young man was from New Mexico and had been hunting with another guide in the Kotzebue area the year before. He was sorely disappointed with his experience, so I was surprised that he booked for this area again. He described his previous experience and I was appalled at the treatment he reported to have received. He was a reasonable and enthusiastic guest and remained so throughout his time with us. He wanted to collect a grizzly and a caribou. His name was Tom.

Our second guest for that final booking period, Brent, was a dairyman from Michigan, a very devout, decent man, seeking a caribou only.

Ron's bull was the best bull of the season for us and a good bull any year.

When I had both new guests at the lodge I noticed fresh caribou meat on the rack and a dandy rack hanging with it. Ron had taken an impressive bull during my absence, which was legal since we had no booked guests in camp and he had purchased a non resident tag.

Shortly after my departure with the Louisiana guests, Ron spotted this fine, well palmated bull across the river. He spent more than two hours trying to get a clear shot and eventually succeeded.

The temperature had dropped below freezing before the southerners departed and the cold weather remained.

In addition to collecting that caribou bull, Ron hand picked several containers of cranberries, blue berries and crow berries with which he made berry bread and a couple of pies which were enjoyed by everyone.

Caribou traffic had been intermittent this entire season, with several days in a row having no sightings. After several days of less than average game activity, Tom decided he preferred to remain at the cabin and glass from the windows. Ron took Brent north with a stiff wind in their faces. Just before eleven that morning I glassed an impressive bull near the top of the moguls of East Bowl Creek. This animal seemed undecided in his movements and after lingering near the skyline, he turned and went back into the canyon. I remained vigilant and after a couple of hours the bull appeared again at the top of the moguls and turned north.

Tom and I got our boots on and walked up creek to intercept him. We shivered in the willows for nearly an hour before Tom had a two hundred yard opportunity to shoot. And he shot well, dropping the beautiful bull on the side hill within sight of the lodge.

Tom was pleased he had elected to hunt from the lodge.

As shadows grew longer, a mob of caribou come out of East Bowl.

This rack has all the components to make it score well, as well as being esthetically pleasing. Its symmetry was nearly perfect, which is rare in caribou. This was the only caribou Tom and I saw that day.

We had it hanging on the meat rack before Ron and Brent returned. They had encountered only some very young bulls in a group of forty cows and calves, but they had seen a large grizzly about five miles northwest of the lodge. Brent announced he planned to apply for a grizzly permit for 2012.

This was a venison meat chili con carne night. Chilli seems to always go down well in cold, windy weather. One must remember to make a big bowl.

Brent had been drawn for a moose permit, but we had not seen any big bulls near the lodge. He was becoming nervous that he might not collect a caribou, either, but he read his bible often and assured himself that he would be successful.

Late the next afternoon we saw several hundred caribou come out of East Bowl canyon and walk rapidly south. I alerted Brent and hustled with him to try to provide him with a shot at a decent bull. But there were no mature bulls in this bunch. Brent had not had good luck on this trip, so I told him he could stay on a few days at no extra fee, since I had no other guests scheduled, plus there was his moose tag to hopefully fill. But after more than an hour in the biting wind he decided to settle on a small bull, rather than risk taking nothing at all.

Probably the least impressive caribou a guest of ours has ever taken.

The next day I took Brent to Kotzebue to catch his scheduled jet flight back to Michigan. He left a day earlier than scheduled. He enthusiastically told me he planned to come again next year. I've often heard that from departing hunters, but I felt like Brent was serious, and in fact he did book for the coming fall and took a grizzly and the number two caribou in the state competition. Persistence often pays dividends.

When I returned to the lodge it was in the low twenties with a clear sky. It was more than ten hours early to change the oil, but I drained it into some empty glass wine jugs which I took to the lodge to use if I needed to start the engine on a cold day with no pre-heating. As I finished the oil drain, a legal bull moose of close to sixty inches in width walked right up the runway and paused to study me at the cub. I counted five points on its lower right palm. It was approaching the rutting time for moose and he was checking out anything that he thought he might breed. If only Brent had stayed to the end of his booking, he would likely have had a chance at that beautiful trophy. How's a guy to know.? One thing for sure is, if you're not in the field and prepared, you'll not get your game.

That left only Ron, Tom and me. Tom had only a grizzly to take.

The frigid wind continued relentlessly from the north. The creeks were icing up. The closest branch of Dipwater Creek went dry. I had the oil stove on at the lodge - not usually necessary, but it was COLD! We were seeing little bands of half a dozen to twenty caribou every day, but Tom was becoming discouraged.

The next morning things warmed up noticeably. Just after supper on the second night after Brent departed, Ron spotted a grizzly walking up the creek. It turned right to put it on a trajectory for the main runway.

We three pulled on our hip boots and warm parkas and hurried to the north end of the runway. Lucky for us, the wind had reversed direction that afternoon and was now coming directly up the creek from the bear to us. This medium sized grizzly was in no hurry as he sniffed and swung his head from right to left. His demeanor was that of a casual shopper in a department store. He no doubt knew about the lodge and maybe thought he would find a morsel to eat thereabouts.

I told Tom to put one up the spout and fill his magazine, giving him four more shots.

As Tom, Ron and I crouched in the low willows, I whispered to Tom to shoot when ready and aim for just below the chin.

The first shot was a solid hit. The bear seemed to jump straight up, then lowered its head to bite at the wound in its brisket.

Tom shot again, it was another hit. This time the bear ran to its left and Tom kept throwing lead at it.

The bear was slowed down and having difficulty maintaining its footing. Before we approached the badly crippled bear I told Tom to fill his magazine again and keep a round in the chamber with the safety engaged.

Finally this bear was completely stilled, Tom had hit him six times with 180 grain bullets from his .300 Winchester magnum. This animal died hard, which was not pleasant for me to endure, but such difficult and prolonged kills are, thankfully, rare.

The pelage on this bear was prime with no rubbed spots. The animal had no noticeable scars.

This boar grizzly was tough to kill.

A larger than usual gall bladder.

Bear gall bladders are of great value to some orientals who use the gall in medicines. Since it became illegal to sell bear galls in Alaska, I normally recover the bladder, hang it to dry, then give it to someone I know, who appreciates it. Its hard to predict the size of any bear's gall bladder. This bear squared just at seven and a half feet and had an extraordinarily large gall bladder.

We had enjoyed another fine season at the lodge - approximately one hundred and fifty-seven miles north of the Arctic circle. Our guests took one Dall ram, ten caribou bulls, three boar grizzlies, some snowshoe hares and willow ptarmigan. All the Arctic char and grayling fish that were caught were released.

The next day I put the cabin temperature oil back in the cub and got Tom, his grizzly hide and gear to town with the caribou rack tied on the right wing struts.

A quick turn around had me back at Trail Creek. Ron had things ready to close up for the winter, so after less than an hour on the ground, we were headed back to Kotzebue. We were happy to feel the warmer conditions.

Ron took the jet back to Colorado and I got the cub to Fairbanks the following day.

This was the last big game animal harvested on Trail Creek in 2011.

2012
The Fall Season

The fall season did not begin well, but it sure could have been a lot worse. After getting the super cub annual done without any complications - other than a twenty foot strip of leading edge fabric delaminating from the left wing during my biannual flight check. Lucky for me, the check pilot was the mechanic who just signed off on the annual. I replaced it in about three hours of cutting, gluing and doping in the hanger.

Then, as so often happens, a huge storm moved in, obscuring visibility from Fairbanks to Kotzebue. Oh well, I spent three days shopping for hard to find items, visiting with friends and doing some reading.

I made the time delay enjoyable - nothing unusual.

Having checked the forecast at the Flight Service Station the evening before, I did not expect to fly that Saturday, but I rolled up my sleeping bag and got ready, just in case. Upon calling up the new charts, I was surprised to see what looked like a narrow window between two large low pressure systems that, if the storms moved as predicted, would allow me to slip across the 440 miles separating where I was from where I wanted to be. If I didn't make it through that narrow window, I would likely be delayed for several more days.

I decided it was good enough for a go.

I stopped at a convenience store to fill my coffee thermos and grab a mini pecan pie. That with my bread, mayonaise, ham and cheese would do fine until I get to Kotzebue. I always carry emergency rations for a trip like that as well.

At Chena Marina airstrip I loaded the cub, topped off the main tanks and filled the belly tank, giving me fuel enough for eight and a half hours of flight time. I also had my "range extender" a plastic bottle that supplements my own internal bladder - it's necessary for long cross country flights without any stops. Once, when able to make the flight directly, it took only four and a quarter hours, but I have spent nearly eight and a half hours on that same trip. The average direct flight takes about six to six and a half hours. The cramped misery would be multiplied, and my bladder unduly stressed, without a range extender.

The first fifty miles went very well. I trimmed the plane for best rate of climb - 72 mph airspeed - and as I ascended past 3,000 feet, my instruments indicated that the quartering left cross wind translated into about a five to eight mile per hour tail wind. That's like money in the bank and reduces the need for frequent use of the range extender, which is a somewhat uncomfortable, pretzeling maneuver from the front seat of a super cub. Performing what for men is normally a stand-up job from a cramped, seated position requires some well practiced contortions, but it beats the alternative. I imagine a monkey attempting to mount a stiff hair brush while in a washing machine, might be an equally graceful sight.

I tuned in my thirty -five year old Automatic Direction Finder (ADF), picked up a Fairbanks radio station and listened to country western music.

Everything going well, I poured myself a cup of coffee and munched down a ham and cheese sandwich, then the pecan pie.

Before I reached the Yukon River I began to encounter light turbulence accompanied by heavy rain. Visibility was good, so I locked onto a GPS heading of 268 degrees, and kept grinding directly westward.

It was warm when I departed Fairbanks - about plus sixty-eight degrees, but as I gained altitude the outside air temperature dropped to plus thirty-four. Wearing only a cotton shirt and having nothing handy to put over that, I pulled the heat lever and the cabin soon was comfortable with steady airflow pouring from the flexible heater hose. Once I was warmed up I stuck the heater hose under my seat. The warm air blowing up my butt felt good and reminded me of previous attendances at political meetings. Citizen voters are expected to feel good with hot air blowing up their butt … right ? It happens in a small aircraft, too.

After about two hours my direct course took me to the Koyukuk river just downstream from the village of Hughs, but the wind blowing from

The Fall Season

140 degrees had become stronger and was now steady at an estimated thirty-five to forty mph with higher gusts and visibility had dropped to about five miles.

Moderate turbulence was steadily thumping me. If I had brought along some dirty laundry in a sealable container with soap it would have received a thorough cycling, - even without an internal agitator.

Realizing that the wind boiling over the mountains west of the Hog River gold mine would make for a really bumpy ride and noticing that the upper half of the mountains was obscured, I flew through the Babantaltlin Hills, then diverted my route to south of the Hogatza range.

It was time to again relieve the bladder before conditions became too demanding for such a distortion, so I did so. It's best to have a bit of altitude and manageable flight command circumstances for such a pretzeling endeavor.

That wind out of the Southeast produced an updraft as it smacked into the terrane, causing me to trim the cub a bit nose down to keep from being pushed up into the overcast and now I was clocking along with my ground speed indicated at 125mph, a full twenty to thirty-one miles faster than my airspeed. All that was good.

Wheeler Creek leads one northwest up a broad, treeless valley to the head of the Selawik River. That route is a "no-no" in overcast conditions during winter time due to the potential for white-outs. With no trees, the snowy surface can be extremely difficult to detect. Today there was no snow, but the rain squalls were so large and dense that I elected to continue on my tack south of the Purcell Mountains. The ceiling and visibility kept dropping, but I needed only about fifteen hundred feet to clear the southern edge of the hills and reach the Selawik flats, so I stayed the course.

Clearing the ridge with a couple hundred feet to spare, I dropped into the flats. Visibility continued to deteriorate and I was getting head winds which reduced my ground speed to 78mph. The extra thirty-two gallons in the belly tank provide a great comfort on any long flight.

Fog went all the way to the ground in places, so I steered north to the winding Selawik River and followed it downstream.

I was able to pick up the Kotzebue Non-Directional Beacon (NDB) about 150 miles out on my ADF. The broadcast indicated conditions were below VFR minimums at that station. I tuned my VHF radio to the Ambler frequency and called to check the weather, but got no response. I switched to the Selawik frequency and again did not make contact. The ceiling remained steady at about 800 feet and visibility varied from less than a mile to about two miles, so I continued on, figuring that if the Kotzebue airport was below minimums when I arrived I could hold outside the control zone for a while until things got good enough for a Special VFR Clearance or I might even land on the beach at Riley Wreck or Seshaulik, each of which is less than ten miles from Kotzebue. Yes, the belly tank full of extra fuel is such a wonderful thing.

My ADF audio was functioning and I noted that conditions were close to those allowing for a "special VFR clearance" to enter the zone and land, so as I crossed Hotham Inlet I called in my position again on the VHF radio and asked for a clearance, hoping to be heard.

"Kotzebue radio, Piper 3421 Papa - west shore inbound, request Special VFR clearance', I said.

That transmission was heard by the Kotzebue Flight Service Station (FSS) and I was given clearance.

"Jake, Kotzebue radio, good to hear you, cleared to enter the zone", or some such thing. I noted that my name was used, rather than my "N" number. Familiarity is comforting.

When I was able to see Kotzebue the wind was blowing Southeast - still 140 degrees at 25 gusting to 48 knots. My rotating beacon, navigation, landing and taxi lights were all on. No other aircraft occupied the zone.

I advised Kotzebue radio that I was on short base leg for runway 180 and intended to land long. My transmission was not answered. My radio was non functional, again.

As I crabbed toward the threshold of the south runway with the wind blowing from the left, I allowed the plane to drift to the right of center of the dirt landing strip. This would allow me to correct a wee bit to the left to slightly reduce the angle of cross wind. Cross winds tend to make aircraft weathercock or turn into the wind, which is counter acted by dropping the upwind aileron, lowering the wing on that side and using the opposite brake as required to hold the roll out straight. Normally one lands on the main wheels, in strong crosswinds, keeping the tail wheel off the ground for better control.

An especially heavy rain squall had reduced visibility and I could not see half way down the runway when my wheels touched. As I let the tail wheel come into contact with the gravel, the cub veered hard to the right which is the opposite of what I expected. I was heading rapidly for the sewer pond just off the right side of the strip. I jammed my heel down hard on the left brake which brought the plane sharply to the left - but with too much speed. I nearly ground looped the aircraft, but luckily did not scrape the right wing tip or otherwise damage the plane. Then I was headed for the ditch on the upwind side of the strip, however the plane was slowing down. I rode both brakes hard with the control stick full back in my lap and came to a stop just short of the drop off. All this action took place in mere seconds, but my mind had traveled through the entire flight training book.

Had I forgotten how to land the durned thing?

I popped open the clam shell door, leaving the engine running on idle, and got out. In the heavy rain I grabbed the handle near the tail and pushed the plane back onto the runway. As I got back in I noticed steam coming from beneath my seat. The driving rain had hit my two brake master cylinders which were so hot they were producing the steam. I'd left the heater hose nozzle right next to the brake cylinders and the fluid had expanded, causing my brakes to be firmly locked. This explained my wild landing. I had never heard of such a thing, but everyone I encountered would hear the story from me. I hoped that no one else would make such an error. Whew! I nearly wrecked the cub three times on that one landing. I felt like I was riding in the palm of God's hand.

With the plane secured in its tie downs, my new priorities were bladder relief and emptying the range extender before anyone arrived to bear witness to either act.

My daughter, Sandy, came out to the field to help me unload and drive me to town. As we passed the Flight Service Station I stopped in to thank them for the clearance and make sure my flight plan was closed. I asked what they thought of my landing, but they said the visibility clamped down just before I landed and they had not been able to see my yellow and black cub much beyond the threshold. I was glad I had intentionally landed long. I did not elaborate on my touch down with the FSS attendants at the time.

Having arrived in Kotzebue on Saturday afternoon, it was sunup on the next Thursday before conditions suitable enough for a trip to the lodge on Trail Creek developed. I made three trips with one passenger each time that day.

We found scant sign of snowshoe hares around the buildings, but that was likely explained by the presence of Lynx. Scat and scratch marks were evident in the yard and a large cat was standing by the door as the first night fell. This was somewhat of a relief to me, as the hares can quickly rebound from heavy predation, but disease can keep their numbers down for many years.

In the spring of 1980 we had more snowshoe hares than I have ever seen before or since, but in April they began to show a bloody diarrhea. I did not see another snowshoe until August, 2005. The night we arrived rain showers resumed and continued for the next six days. We spent most of the time inside the buildings. It was not what we had come for, but it beat being stuck in Kotzebue.

The following Wednesday I transported one guest, Joey Coyle, back to Kotzebue and the following day met the two incoming guests. One was Brent from the previous season, the other was Lloyd who had hunted with me on three previous occasions. We sat until Saturday before weather conditions allowed me to get them to the lodge on September 1.

September second dawned with rain and fog. We enjoyed a hearty breakfast and as we lingered in the main room, someone spotted a herd of about one hundred and eighty Caribou coming down the east side of the valley. This band was comprised of mostly cows and calves with three young bulls and two large trophy bulls bringing up the rear. They had come out of Break Ankle Canyon and side-hilled just east of the lodge, almost within rifle range, but moving at a rapid clip.

Ron and Brent took off across the swamp in hopes of getting a shot, but they returned after two hours. The animals were just moving too fast. We were enjoying bowls of warm soup when I glassed a good bear feeding on berries on the north slope of Three Mile Ridge, down creek from the lodge. The rain had stopped and visibility was good. Our guest hunter, Brent, Ron and I set off immediately toward the bear.

We used walking sticks to assist in fording the rain swollen channels of Trail Creek, leaving the sticks on the far bank. When we had walked to within a mile of the last known location of the bear, we could no longer see it. We sat near the bank of the stream, focused on the berry littered hillside until after about a half hour, Ron detected what he thought was the top of the bear's back. When I located his mark, I agreed that it was the bear, lying just across a small drainage. We struck off at a fast walk.

The wind was steady at ten to twelve miles per hour down the valley. We were upwind, but about two hundred feet lower elevation than the bear. I was confident that we could go straight for the bruin with little risk of it winding us.

Over the years I have come to realize that bears eyesight is much better than most people think. And all bears know their country well. To avoid exposing ourselves as we moved along the edge of an open alluvial fan, even though it was a half mile from the bear, we chose a route that forced us to claw our way across a steep, muddy cut bank of the river. A slip there would have landed us in the rushing water, but a glimpse of us skylined on the edge of the fan would possibly have resulted in the bear seeing us and disappearing into the brush choked draw just beyond the meadow in which it was feeding.

The last thousand yards to the bear were mostly knee high brush with a few taller bushes and some shallow draws. We used the cover as best we could and finally were within 350 yards of the bear which was once again up and feeding.

We needed to close the range as much as possible, so I sent Ron in front with Brent close behind and me bringing up the rear. We proceeded very slowly and stayed close behind each other in order to make only one silhouette, in case the bear looked our way and detected something amiss.

Daylight was threatening to close down our operation if the shot was not made soon. The dark Grizzly began to move more rapidly toward the brushy draw and was only one hundred yards from the cover when I told Brent he would have to make his shot. The range by then was around 225 yards. I recorded the event with my video camera. The sound of the first bullet impacting the bear was unmistakable. Immediately, the beast rolled and nipped at itself, not knowing what had bitten it. My impression was that the shot was a bit aft of ideal, a bit toward the stern side - euphemisms aside, it was a gut shot.

"Shoot him again, Brent," I hollered.

I sensed the second shot was a miss and told Ron to help. The wounded bear was running full stride for the heavy cover.

Once a bear has been hit, it is our practice to have the guest hunter keep shooting it until it lies motionless, or if it appears to be escaping, Ron or I may assist in putting it down.

The Grizzly disappeared into the tangled vegetation without another shot being fired.

Then I realized that both Ron and I had been filming. That was my mistake as I should have made sure that one of us was ready to shoot if necessary.

With the wind still steady from the north, I walked around the lower end of the brush and told Ron to take Brent to the upper end after giving me fifteen minutes to get set up on the downwind side. I was hoping that with some good luck, the bear would smell the two men and come out downwind, allowing me to dispatch it. This bear, like most wounded bruins, remained holed up in the dense thicket.

After thirty minutes Ron left Brent in position with a good view, cautioning him to shoot only if the bear came out in the clear on his side, but under no circumstances was he to shoot into the brushy draw.

When Ron and I met, I told him that there was time enough for me to make one criss crossing shashay down through the draw in hopes of locating the bear. If the bear was dead, we would have a difficult time finding it, but I was confident that it was gut shot and would be plenty lively ... and angry. If I did not rouse the bear in one downhill transit we would have to come back in the morning.

"Boss, how 'bout I go through the brush with you?", asked Ron.

In my 45 years of guiding in Alaska I have dug numerous wounded bears out of dense thickets, but never allowed anyone to come along. I'd much rather risk a mauling than being shot by accident with a soft nosed hunting bullet. But this thicket was large and two people working it seemed a better idea, especially since Ron is cool natured and absolutely dependable.

"Ron, that is a capital idea! We should try to remain within twenty to thirty yards of each other and keep in frequent voice contact. The noise will no doubt hold the bear's attention and coming from two sources, I believe it will confuse the beast and hopefully prevent it from making a well calculated rush on either of us. So, partner, let's do it!", I replied.

We each put a round in the chamber and checked that our magazines had three more.

I told Ron that in circumstances such as these, the bear always comes low and fast, sometimes without making any sounds, but other times it begins with a grunt or a "wuff." It would be necessary for us to bend over low to see under some spots. The bear was dark colored and would be difficult to see in the diminishing light. If either of us needed to get on our hands and knees to go through some of the densest thickets, we were to advise the other before beginning to crawl. I told Ron that I was not going to lift my scope covers as shooting, if it came to that, would be fast at extremely close range and barrel sighting would be all that time would allow. I told him to be careful and wished him good luck.

We began our slow, noisy journey down slope through the tangle of willows, dwarf birch, grass and blueberry growth. A single willow ptarmigan flushed close by me, which gave me a twitch, and a spike in my blood pressure, no doubt. Ron had a similar experience - buggered by a bird. We both heard single birds flush out downhill and ahead of us. We reckoned the bear had frightened the birds and focused on the area from which the noise came.

After about ten minutes of tense back and forth transecting, Ron was to my left when he yelled "BEAR" before shooting two times. The bear came busting through the brush toward me. I got a shot into the right front shoulder and another into the right ham as the bear continued past me and downhill. The bear's route was about fifteen yards from me. I paused to put two more bullets in my magazine.

We came together to compare notes. Ron said he saw the bear just off to his left side and about ten yards distant. As it came toward him he tried to brain shoot it. He hit it in the head, but missed the second shot.

Ron moved to the right side of my position and we resumed our slow search. When I came to a ditch of about eight feet in depth and fifteen feet wide, I hollered to Ron that I was near the bank of a deep ditch and I was uncomfortable with the situation. As I eased into the bottom of the ditch the bear immediately growled and wuffed three times, then rose up atop the opposite bank and turned toward me. I sighted down the barrel, aiming for the point of the jaw, but hit it in the neck, spinning it around. As it proceeded downhill, Ron hit it twice in the body.

Once more we reloaded our rifles. This time Ron had a good visual fix on where he last saw the bear, so we proceeded in that direction.

Again it got up on all fours and I put a bullet into the spine, rolling the bear. It stopped against a willow bush at the lower end of the thicket and thrashed a few seconds before going still. It was sudden death overtime for the Grizzly and I became aware of a sudden, profound silence.

Ron and I shook hands, reloaded our magazines and made sure the chambers were empty, then called to Brent to come.

Ron's first shot had blown out the upper and lower canine teeth and the cheek on the right side. My first shot broke the right humerus, the second entered the right ham, but hit no bones. My third shot struck the left side of the neck, missing the spine. Ron's third and forth shots were into the chest cavity and my last shot severed the spine just behind the front shoulder. It took eight shots to kill this one.

The dark Grizzly was a female with mature, developed nipples, but no sign of nursing cubs. Three days later, after fleshing, it squared nose to tail 7'3" and claw tip to claw tip 7'5", giving it a square measurement of 7'4." Its skull measured 21 12/16 inches. The silvertip hide was in ideal condition, being well furred with no sign of rubbing.

Brent was ecstatic. He was full of wonder and praise at the conditions and outcome of this first day of his hunt. He said that he had been praying for us when we were in the brush after the wounded bear and was so relieved that we had found it and neither of us was injured.

I suggested that it might be appropriate to now offer our thanks for the successful and dramatic conclusion of our endeavors. We three did that. Light was fading fast, so after making photographs, we peeled the hide off, removed the hind quarters and the gall bladder to take back to camp and

Ron Phillips and Brent Wilson with Brent's big sow.

loaded Ron's pack board and mine for the walk back. We arrived at the lodge an hour and a half later. I offered to make some super. As often happens at the end of a day like this, no one seemed especially hungry, so we snacked on smoked salmon with crackers and popcorn. Lloyd had remained at the lodge and reported that two more groups of Caribou had come through using the same trail as the first herd of the day. Each mob had forty to fifty animals, but no outstanding bulls were among them. We ended that day with a refreshing whiskey over ice.

September 3 opened with a temperature of plus twenty-nine, north wind of about ten miles per hour with occasional gusts to twenty-five in rain.

A band of approximately seventy-five Caribou came out of Break Ankle Canyon and traced the footsteps of the previous day's migrants. Before noon a herd of about three hundred animals came through. This group had a couple dozen mature bulls, one of which carried remarkably well palmated antlers. We four struck off as fast as we could boot up and go, but the animals were moving too fast for us.

The rain continued, so we returned to the lodge and enjoyed mugs of hot coffee and snacks. About 1:30pm more Caribou came out of Break Ankle canyon and joined the others, making a mass of about five hundred animals scattered over the moguls at the mouth of East Bowl canyon. They were only from one quarter to three quarters of a mile from the lodge.

About six o'clock in the evening a band containing more than a dozen good bulls laid down near the cutback off the end of the runway. With the breeze at our back, we hustled to the base of the cut bank and eased our way toward the relaxed animals. When we rounded the last corner, the bulls were gone, so I took Brent up the cut bank and saw the bulls quartering away from us at about one hundred twenty yards distance. All the mature bulls were of similar antler quality, so to minimize the chance of picking a lesser one, I told Brent to shoot the last one in the string of animals.

His shot was high -because he held high - after I told him to just aim for what he wanted to hit and to squeeze the trigger lovingly - not to jerk it!

The Caribou were now trotting away and disappeared in a small swale. I told my guest to hold for my instructions on which to shoot at ... again.

When the string of animals emerged from the depression, none showed signs of having been hit, so I told Brent to take the big bull that was third from the end. This time the bull gave a bit of a lurch, followed by the distinctive "bung" sound of a gut shot. With the large group of animals now running, there was no opportunity for another clear shot. I shut down the video camera and visually followed the animals' movement toward the higher ground to the east. Using my binoculars I maintained a good fix on where the wounded bull was located in the mob.

I sent Ron and Lloyd back the way we'd come to hopefully head off the herd if they turned to the north. Brent and I moved into the swale and crouched down to watch and wait.

Within minutes another large band of Caribou came trotting in from the north. Upon sighting the new group of animals, the band with the wounded bull turned West to join them. As the two groups met they stopped and milled around. Though I scrutinized the milling mass of

The Fall Season

animals carefully, I could not pick out our cripple. I told Brent there would be no more shooting until we had that bull located and on the ground.

Some of the Caribou went back to feeding while others nervously glanced about for whatever had startled them. The group remained in the same location, so Brent and I approached them, bent over and walking slowly. I lifted the butt end of my rifle high over my head and moved it about, making no attempt to hide, hoping to appear like a feeding bull with a large antler. The Caribou were upwind from us. Their curiosity overcame them and they came toward us at a trot - stopping a mere sixty yards off. A few cows began to move past us, then turned south to get our scent. Still, I could not spot the wounded bull. Once the downwind cows got our smell they snorted and turned, trotting off down creek. The biggest bunch of Caribou turned toward the eastern foothills. Finally I picked out the injured bull which was following a group of seven others, but as they gained elevation, he fell further and further behind. I told Brent that we must keep him in sight and I was confident that we could finish him off. As the string of bulls crested and topped over the skyline, the cripple began

Brent with his first Caribou trophy at the lodge.

turning round and round and finally laid down in a spot we could easily keep in sight. He would soon be ours!

The coups de grace was delivered by Brent from forty yards. It was a good bull and I felt especially good that it had not become the first wounded Caribou that I have ever lost.

As we took pictures and butchered the bull, other Caribou came streaming by, oblivious to our presence and activities.

As we returned to the lodge three mature bulls came on a path to intersect our route. Brent had a second tag ready to use so we maneuvered to make that possible. At sixty yards, Brent shot his second bull of the day - and a good shot and day it had been.

Everyone was back at the lodge just after eleven in the evening and ready for a meal. The pot of bear stew was delicious.

September 4 began with drizzle and +34 degrees, but with Caribou visible in all quadrants from the lodge windows everything seemed wonderful! All four of us searched the various herds for impressive racks.

It was a day to please the most picky of hunters. Patience and discrimination would surely be rewarded. Lloyd had hunted with me several times in the past thirty years, taking two Grizzlies, two bull Moose and several Sitka Blacktail deer on Kodiak Island. His primary focus this time was a really big Caribou … and a Wolf if the opportunity arose. Another Grizzly was a possibility, as he had a permit, but a bear was not high on his list this year.

After several hours of careful glassing from the main room of the lodge, locating potential targets with the binoculars, followed by closer examination with the "long eye" (my 15 to 60 power Bausch and Lomb spotting scope on a heavy tripod) … and hints of developing eyestrain, I found a bull that would tempt even the most demanding of hunters. This animal wore antlers with nicely palmated uppers showing more than seven points on each side, outstanding bez with seven long tines bilaterally, and two well developed double shovels. In a group of about sixty animals which included several other eye catching bulls, he was clearly the greatest of the gang. He might well turn out to be the best bull of the year. When you see an animal of this quality, long before all the tines are evaluated, you know it's a taker for sure.

The band he was with laid down and did not move for a couple of hours. They were resting in the middle of a large alluvial fan two miles Northwest of the lodge. Putting Lloyd within reasonable shooting range would be a challenge. At 2:30 pm I sent Ron with Lloyd to stalk the big bull as I began to flesh Brent's Grizzly and Brent cut meat away from the skull.

After five hours of steady fleshing I had the bear skin ready for salting. On short breaks from his work on the skull, Brent had been keeping track of our friends from the window. We never heard the shot, but just before 8:00 pm we saw the big bull go down. The herd charged away down country toward the lodge.

Figuring it would take a couple of hours for the boys to return with the meat and trophy, I began to cook a big pot of spaghetti sauce.

About 10:00 pm Ron and Lloyd came in with that dandy bull, all the meat, and tired bodies. We dined on the remainder of the bear stew,

Lloyd with the beautiful bull Caribou.

spaghetti, salad and fresh chocolate cake. It had been another productive day - the third such in a row. The meat poles were laden with prime eating, hides were salted and our world was right.

September 5 dawned with a high overcast, a north wind of ten to fifteen miles per hour and a warm + 42 degrees. As we were shoving breakfast down our necks a herd of approximately three hundred Caribou came out of East Bowl and turned south down Trail Creek. Seeing no remarkably good bulls in that bunch, we hiked up into the eastern foothills for better coverage of the valley.

The wind had grown tired, it seemed. In the calm, cool evening air we watched several short eared owls harvest lemmings from the swamp. A couple of snow shoe hares came close to the buildings to nibble at salt that had fallen from the hides.

A hearty dinner of barbequed caribou ribs, corn, salad and freshly baked cake put us all into a drowsy mood and we hit the racks early. Gentle belches of the percolator brewing our coffee were the only sounds the next morning as our guests came up to see the heavy fog which hid even the outbuildings from our view.

Hints of break up of the nebulous cover began around ten and by noon the fog was lifting in spots. A slight southerly breeze cleared off the foothills and soon we were free of the damp obscuration.

Brent had been drawn for a Moose permit, so he and I headed down toward Popple Creek which often holds those giant deer this time of year. Ron and Lloyd hiked up creek to see what might be available.

We spotted twelve Caribou running across West Bowl fan with a bull in the lead. They were obviously spooked. Anytime I see a bull Moose or Caribou running in front of a band of cows in the fall time, I think … "Wolf" … and it usually proves to be the cause of this abnormal behavior. The Caribou dropped into the willows of Trail Creek and came toward us. Brent was wishing that he could take another one, but his legal limit had been reached. Brent told me he thought he heard a shot. Secretly I wondered if he was fantasizing. As the first Caribou came within two hundred yards of us, another group of forty with two very good bulls traced the same route.

Leaving Brent to continue glassing, I went back to the lodge to fillet a salmon for supper.

A light rain had set in, so I placed plastic tarps over the racks to protect our hanging winter meat. As I began to prepare the salmon, in came Ron and Lloyd with the first load of meat from a large Caribou. Brent had indeed heard a shot. After first spotting a white and a grey Wolf, the pair of hunters had seen the larger band of Caribou. It looked like the wolves had given up on the ungulates and headed north at a fast pace, so they maneuvered to get within range and Lloyd took his second big bull. This animal had a longer main beam, a massive body, and was good all around - not quite so impressive as his first - but a taker, anytime.

As I prepared supper, Lloyd and Ron retrieved the rest of the meat, the cape and rack of his trophy.

After supper we took all took a much needed sauna, Ron and I did some personal laundry. We were ready to call it a day when my last survey with binoculars revealed a large Grizzly coming over three mile ridge toward the berry patch that had given us Brent's bear. It was too near dark for us

Lloyd with his second Caribou

to act on it, but I figured it would remain in the area, feeding on the rich berry patches.

We retired with the warm satisfaction of another good day and the possibility of Lloyd taking a Grizzly in the morning. September 7 began with a soaker rain shower. We scrutinized Three Mile Ridge and all the berry patches between there and the lodge, as well as those well upstream, expecting to sight the big Grizzly, but he did not show. At one point someone hollered "Bear!" but it turned out to be a big porcupine. Those herbivores have a rolling saunter similar to that of a large bear and have fooled me countless times in the past. I once walked about three miles to check out one such "bear" that had ambled out of sight, only to discover a bristle pig. Dall sheep had descended to feeding areas just above the willows. I guessed they had not scented Wolves recently and may be using this opportunity to savor some of the lower level delectables before freeze up.

Several dense flights of Willow Ptarmigan came down the valley and landed close to the lodge just before dark.

Color changes in the leaves of dwarf birch, blue berry bushes and cottonwood trees were remarkably advanced since the last time we noticed. Most years the leaves undergo an extreme color metamorphosis during the third week of August, which was delayed by more than two weeks this season, so it seemed the onset of winter may be delayed for this year.

As sunlight reached the valley on Saturday, September 8, with an outside temperature of plus twenty degrees, I watched frost form and grow in the clear, cold air. The newly generated frost would last for a couple of hours but was thick enough to provide tracking assistance until it melted away. Any tracks we saw in the frost would be freshly made. This was the first clear sky day I had seen since August 3. Morning sunlight hit the lodge at 11:45 am and soon dissolved the frost.

Ron and Lloyd walked north to glass some of the berry patches not visible from the lodge. Brent and I went south in hopes of locating a good bull moose for him. By mid afternoon we were at the rain swollen, icy East Bowl Creek. I looked around for a willow from which to cut walking sticks, but seeing none close by, I imprudently decided to go it without the aid of a third leg. Large boulders normally make secure stepping stones, but this year slick green moss covered most of them. As I was nearing the far side of the creek I slipped off a rock and plunged into a four foot deep hole, as I struggled to stand in the swift current and slippery rocks, I dowsed myself again. I was soaked and had submerged my rifle. Rats!

Brent from the other bank, offered to come to my assistance, but I told him to keep clear of the slick rocks and sloshed my way back to him.

Once ashore, I sat on a tussock and removed my boots, then poured the water out and quickly put them back on, as I could feel my socks beginning to freeze in the cold air. I disassembled the bolt of my Winchester Model 70, dried it and checked it for function.

I pointed out a high place from which to glass and told Brent to go there and glass for a couple of hours, making sure to return well before dark. If he saw a Moose with desirable antlers, he could shoot it, but only if it had at least four points on at least one of the brow shovels. There was no need for him to lose the chance of sighting his quarry.

As I hustled back I noticed some different looking lichens, so I pocketed samples for delivery to the National Park Service and the Alaska Department of Fish and Game. They could key them out and I would learn what they were.

I set a brisk pace back to the lodge and was in the yard in less than an hour. Soaked or not, due to my exertion, I was not suffering from the cold. I stripped off my clothes, wrung them out and hung them against the walls of the lodge and sauna building which felt warm to the touch in the afternoon sunlight. Before I got into dry shorts and under shirt, the chill had left me.

Transient lichen. *(Masonhalea richardsonii)*

Again I disassembled the bolt of my Model 70, dried the rifle off with paper towels and oiled everything. This was not the first soaking for that fine old piece ... or for me.

A small plane flew over and I recognized my friend Charles Dixon, who landed. I pulled on some britches and went to meet him. He accepted my invitation to stay the night with us.

I stoked up the sauna and began the supper of chicken fried Caribou, mashed potatoes and gravy, with salad and cranberry dessert.

Ron and Lloyd came in, having seen nine Caribou, but no bear. Brent reported seeing only Caribou cows and calves. The sauna felt good and we all hit our bags at 11:00pm.

Sunday, September 9 dawned clear and cold at plus fifteen degrees. I had scheduled a trip to Kotzebue to deliver Lloyd and pick up our incoming hunter, David, but with such great hunting conditions and having seen the big Grizzly just two days before I decided to delay one day, so I called in an extension of my flight plan by 24 hours and called the incoming hunter to let him know the schedule. Brent was interested an a flight seeing excursion. Charles had agreed to take him, so off they went. Ron and Lloyd headed down creek to the South Overlook.

I used the day to fill my bear attracting plastic bottles with creosote. Hung around the buildings on a wire or string, bears can't resist biting them and since 1975, these attractants are probably why we had no serious damage to the cabins by bears - until 2014. I hang a couple dozen or more every year. Completing the bottling chore, I cut some willows from the runway and sawed up some dried wood for the sauna stove.

Upon their return, Brent and Charles reported seeing seven Caribou at the head of Trail Creek, while Ron and Lloyd spotted only one porcupine and some sheep.

For dinner we enjoyed baked chicken, macaroni and cheese, salad and fresh carrot cake.

Monday was our third day with visibility clear and unlimited. We loaded Charles airplane with about 400 pounds of meat. I took Lloyd with his antlers and gear and we departed about noon thirty. We flew directly on the GPS and landed in less than an hour and a half. It was a rush to get Lloyd's antlers crated for shipment, but he checked in and got on his jet. Someone had pilfered gas from my five hundred gallon tank, so I would need to get more at the bulk plant in the morning. David, the incoming hunter, was very patient and spent the night with me in the sod shack.

At the post office I ran into a friend who was planning to visit a buddy of mine in Nevada, so I handed him some prime Caribou backstraps to carry south.

Dropping the lichen samples off with both the Federal and State offices, I later learned it was a "transient lichen", which grows on the surface without roots - what a curious thing! In forty-five years, I had never noticed one before. The other was a spore bearing lichen, also new to me.

David and I departed Kotzebue for the lodge about 4pm. The flight was pleasant with no turbulence and we saw about sixty sheep on the Eli River and Trail Creek.

After sighting in David's rifle and making a shot with mine, we dined on chili and hit the hay after midnight.

Wednesday, September 12 began with a high overcast and +22 degrees. Ron and Brent went down creek to fish while I took David to the East Moguls to glass for whatever we might see. We saw only sheep. Brent caught both Arctic Char and Grayling.

About 3pm a Cessna 206 landed and two men got out. It was a local charter plane and I later learned that a State Fish and Game inspector had come to check licenses, etc. We watched them from our glassing position. They missed us this time, but there was nothing amiss, anyway.

Dinner this time was pressure cooked, barbequed Caribou ribs, potatoes and fresh chocolate cake.

The next day, after bacon, biscuits and gravy, Ron and Brent walked to the South Overlook for Moose or Wolves, but saw only sheep.

David and I went north and half a mile from the lodge encountered eleven Caribou. The only bull in the bunch was a young one and I encouraged David to hold his fire in expectation of a better trophy. We walked on past the Bear Stairs and glassed for two hours in a chilly north wind. The same band of Caribou walked just below us, heading north. Had I to do it over, I would have let David shoot the young bull, but this was not the first time I had a hunter hold off, only to not get another opportunity.

Snowshoe hares had been on a rapid population increase from 2005 through 2011, but this year they were in short supply. Frequent Lynx sign and the one sighting we made in the yard probably explained the hare shortage. Over predation normally is followed by a decrease in the local carnivore numbers and a rapid rebound of hares. I hope we see that take place in this cycle. We spotted only three hares this day.

Brent had remained past the normal twelve day booking in hopes of taking a Moose. He had been with us in 2011 when a dandy bull walked by the lodge on September 15, but this year, Moose sign was scarce and we had not seen a single one. He decided he would just go home on September 14. I didn't argue the point, but did mention that another day or two might pay off. It was a long shot, of course. It would have worked the year before, but....

Saturday, September 14 began as another calm, clear, cold day. The thermometer indicated +18 degrees. We enjoyed a good breakfast of scrambled eggs and salmon hash. We glassed from the lodge, loaded the cub and departed about 1:00 pm. I took a short sashay up Trail Creek, but saw only sheep. We turned south, popped over the ridge to the Kuguroruk River and after crossing the Noatak River we flew down the Miumerak Creek. The locals refer to a couple of mountain lakes that I used to camp on as "Jake's Lakes." They were calm and beautiful this crisp fall day. Sheep were out in large numbers and feeding low on the slopes, but we saw no Moose or Caribou.

After getting Brent confirmed for his early morning departure and purchasing three large fish shipping containers, I did some grocery shopping before heading to the shack. We took our dinner at the hospital restaurant and returned to crate his antlers and pack his hides and meat. We were tucked into our beds before ten o'clock.

As we got Brent checked in for the Alaska Airlines flight the next morning at 6:30am, the terminal was loaded with hunters in new camouflage outfits - Cabela people. None but Brent had any meat or trophies to check in. As we waited for the jet to arrive, several fellows came to ask us where we had found the animals, as they had seen none. I passed out several of my business cards, but most of these Americans would not consider a fully guided hunt, opting for the seemingly less expensive "drop-off" Transported services.

Most of the Transporter trips wind up costing the guest hunters more money for five to seven days of hunting from a tent than I charge for a twelve day guided trip from the lodge, and success rates for the high volume operations are only about fifteen percent. But the people think they're getting it on the cheap. Oh well.

It seems there's plenty of irksome things to deal with in Kotzebue and I am always glad to climb back in the cub and get out of town.

A dark, ragged overcast had moved in making my trip north turbulent and wet as I flew through several big rain and snow squalls, but Trail Creek was nearly calm and dry.

It was time to change the oil in the airplane, so I took advantage of the nice conditions and the warm engine to drain out the old lubricant for use in the sauna stove and set seven quarts of new oil in the lodge for putting in warm whenever I decided to fly again. As I finished up at the airplane a large bull Moose came strolling up the runway making his plosive grunts as he walked. He was looking for love and oblivious to me and the aircraft. Oh man, I wished that Brent had remained for this. He would have been ecstatic at an opportunity for such a beast and we would have had nearly no meat packing to do, as well as an abundance of fine eating for the coming winter. This was a duplicate of the previous year! Murphy rides with us all and I'm sure ole Murph was giggling at me ... and Brent.

Sunday, September 16 came with clear skies, plus twenty degrees and a north wind of fifteen to twenty miles per hour. North of us the heavy overcast was depositing snow and by mid afternoon, visibility was reduced to a quarter of a mile with snow covering everything. Late in the day we saw another bull moose walk up the strip and pass within ten yards of the airplane. That was rubbing it in, for sure. As we got ready to retire a hard rain noisily pelted the roof.

———

Monday broke with a four thousand foot overcast, plus thirty degrees and a light north wind. Most of the snow was gone from the valley floor, but it remained at five hundred feet and above. By noon we were getting a south wind at fifteen to twenty miles per hour with drizzle and fog. David took a three hour nap after lunch. Ron and I puttered around with preparations for closing the lodge for winter. I cooked up a batch of spaghetti and after telling some stories and reading we all went to bed.

———

The south wind remained steady into the next morning and brought a new cover of snow. We three walked up to the East Moguls to glass for about three hours but saw only sheep and a couple large flocks of ptarmigan. We were back in the lodge by 7:00pm for baked chicken, vegetables and cake.

———

Wednesday revealed a new layer of snow, followed by a steady rain throughout the rest of the day. We enjoyed the comforts of the lodge and made use of the library. We were all thankful to not be out on a flooding gravel bar in a tent.

———

Thursday, September 21 we awoke to thick fog, making it impossible to see the sauna building fifty yards from the lodge. Shortly after noon, as the fog began to lift, we climbed again to the East Moguls to look for game, but it seemed nothing was moving. This was a damp and chilly day with no encouragement from any animals so we went back to the lodge at 5:00pm. The broadcast radio said heavy rains were causing sever flooding in the Delta, Susitna, Talkeetna and Matanuska rivers. Some bridges were washed out.

The local radio reported that a resident of Kiana had shot my friend and aircraft mechanic, Paul Buckle, and his brother in their tent camp on the Squirrel River. The shooter used Paul's .44 magnum pistol, hitting both men in the chest, then fled down the river in their boat, leaving them for dead. The next day, Paul was able to get a radio distress call out and the badly wounded men were picked up and flown to Kotzebue. The shooter was still on the loose.

Friday morning the dense fog was back, but it began to lift by 9:00 am. I spotted a large grey wolf on the west alluvial fan. It appeared to be searching for rodents. I suggested to David that we try to get within range for a shot, but he was more interested in not missing his jet flight home, so we departed about noon. I told Ron he was free to try to take that wolf, if he wanted to do so, as soon as we departed.

Fog was still patchy - heavy in places - and was dense at the squeeze spot on Trail Creek west of Misheguk Mountain. I lowered flaps and proceeded down stream with better vertical than horizontal visibility, then broke out after about two miles. At the mouth of Trail Creek we spotted three large bull Muskoxen being stalked by a huge Grizzly. The bovines were aware of the bear and had their rumps together. That bear would have been a dandy to collect. Fog was still patchy thick, so I flew through the Noatak flats to town.

After getting David squared away in a local bed and breakfast I went back up for Ron. Rain, snow and fog still had the direct route socked in so I went through the flats again. I didn't take time to look for the large Grizzly near the three muskoxen.

Ron had lost sight of the wolf shortly after we left, so he went about getting the place ready to close up. We were soon back in the air. With no meat or hides to haul, the cub was quickly off the ground.

This time the lower Trail Creek was more open and we saw seven large bull Muskoxen all bunched up with a medium sized Toklat Grizzly on one side and a cream colored bear on the other. This was only about six miles from the lodge - a shame it had not taken place earlier and closer to the lodge. We landed on runway 18 in Kotzebue just at dark.

After grabbing a burger to go, we unloaded our gear and went to Paul Buckle's house to hear the latest on that issue. Several guides and Transporters had gathered and the whiskey was flowing. Paul's brother was in worse shape, but both had been flown to an Anchorage hospital and full recovery was expected for each of them. The mood was extremely angry and some mentioned lynching the shooter who had been apprehended and was in the local jail. I figured it was time for Ron and me to go home.

Saturday the twenty-second opened nice in Kotzebue. For several years I'd been planning to take Ron up to the Wullik River for some fresh sea-run Arctic Char. Normally the big, fat trout are stacked up like cord wood in the holes and strike voraciously at artificial lures or flies. The night before, the aviation outlook forecast was for strong winds north of town, so after hearing that Kivalina was blowing NE 30, gusting to 40, we drove down to the Flight Service station, where we learned that the report was correct. It was already turbulent and promised to get much worse. So, once again, our fishing trip would have to be cancelled.

A Transporter friend called to say he had a bunch of Caribou meat to distribute. We stopped by, most of what remained was badly bloodshot, but we took it and dropped it off to some elderly people who appreciated it. As Ron secured his stand-by seat on the evening Alaska Airlines jet, I drained about 60 gallons of fuel out of my big tank into small containers to be stored in the vans. Left in the large tank, it would likely disappear over the winter and I've never liked the idea of providing fuel for thieves.

After Ron's departure I did some paperwork for ADF&G on licenses and tag sales, then hit the sack. The wind had picked up to about thirty mph and was quite noisy.

Sunday morning, after checking the airplane, I drove down to the Episcopal Church to hear my old friend Wilfred Lane deliver his sermon. Wilfred is as fine an example of a true Christian as I have known. He had several bouts with brain cancer and showed serious scars on his head. He had been ill again this summer and most people expected him to meet his maker soon. As I walked in at the ringing of the bell, Wilfred was at the door, took my hand and said "Jake, we've been waiting for you."

"I'm sorry to be late, my friend."

Wilfred smiled as he said "Jake, it's never too late, old friend."

There were only six people in attendance, which has become the norm, unfortunately. This morning's sermon was about baptism and at the conclusion, Wilfred asked, "Jake, are you ready ?" With no hesitation, I said, "Yes, I am ready."

What a moving experience! Wilfred said this might prove to be his last baptism and he was so happy that it was me. But he added that we, were all in God's hands.

We enjoyed some cookies and coffee after the ceremony and I drove Wilfred and his wife, Vivian home.

Normally I would have switched from my Borer (high performance) prop to my cruise prop, but it was windy and cold and looked like I may be stuck in Kotzebue for several days, so I got organized for closing up the shack and departing when conditions permitted.

The old '77 ford pickup quit, due to a solenoid short, which ate up a couple hours that chilly afternoon, but with the help of my friend, John Rae, I got it running.

Monday passed quickly with local chores, mailing in payments to various places and some visiting. The four o'clock forecast indicated I might be able to get to Fairbanks the next day, Tuesday, which would be nice.

Tuesday came with plus thirty degrees, calm conditions and a skiff of new snow, as well as an extremely adherent layer of frost coating the plane. I broomed and roped off the wings and control surfaces several times, then decided I should turn the cub to pick up the sunlight to clear the frost. Removing the frost took over two hours, but I took off at 11:15am. I was able to climb to 9,500 feet where the outside air temperature was +18 degrees, beneath a high, dark overcast to the east. I was comfortably dressed and the heater made it a pleasant flight. From Kobuk Lake I could see Purcell Mountain, and once there, the Hogatza Range and Indian Mountain were visible. The visibility remained remarkable good all the way to Chena Marina, where I landed at 4:45pm. Headwinds had slowed me down by as much as 20mph in places, but five and a half hours for that 440 mile trip is not bad. My airspeed indicated 92 to 95mph, but ground speed averaged only 80mph. I drained the hot oil and unloaded the cub.

I picked up my eighteen year old daughter Bess at her University of Alaska dorm and we enjoyed a Mexican dinner and a good visit.

Wednesday was active with getting pickling oil and running the engine for fifteen minutes to soak everything with the preservative. I ran a quick check on compression and all cylinders were good. A quick shower at the Fairbanks International Airport pilot lounge - a wonderful facility - which would be welcome in every airport, and a haircut had me ready for dinner again with Bess.

The next day I drove the truck to Anchorage to spend two days with my long time friend, Jim Cann, before driving down to Homer to catch the ferry to Kodial. It had been an imperfect, but good season.

In December 2013 I learned that Lloyd's bull ranked first place and Brent's was number two in the 2012 Annual Big Three Competition.

www.ingramcontent.com/pod-product-compliance
Lightning Source LLC
Chambersburg PA
CBHW071837230426
43671CB00012B/1986